A PREFACE
TO ECONOMIC
DEMOCRACY

ABOUT
QUANTUM
BOOKS

QUANTUM, THE UNIT OF
EMITTED ENERGY. A QUANTUM
BOOK IS A SHORT STUDY
DISTINCTIVE FOR THE AUTHOR'S
ABILITY TO OFFER A RICHNESS OF
DETAIL AND INSIGHT WITHIN
ABOUT ONE HUNDRED PAGES
OF PRINT. SHORT ENOUGH TO BE
READ IN AN EVENING AND
SIGNIFICANT ENOUGH
TO BE A BOOK.

Robert A. Dahl

A Preface
to Economic
Democracy

University of California Press

Berkeley   Los Angeles

University of California Press
Berkeley and Los Angeles, California
© 1985 by
The Regents of the University of California

LIBRARY OF CONGRESS CATALOGING
IN PUBLICATION DATA

Dahl, Robert Alan, 1915–
    A preface to economic democracy.
    Bibliography: p.
    Includes index.
    1. Employee ownership—United States. 2. Management—
United States—Employee participation. 3. Equality—
United States. 4. Democracy. 5. Liberty. I. Title.
HD5660.U5D34   1985   338.6   84-8483
ISBN 0-520-05877-1 (alk. paper)

Printed in the United States of America

10   09   08   07   06   05   04   03   02
14   13   12   11   10   9   8   7   6

The paper used in this publication meets the minimum requirements
of ANSI/NISO Z39.48-1992 (R 1997) (*Permanence of Paper*). ∞

Contents

Acknowledgments

I should like to express my appreciation to the University of California, Berkeley, for the opportunity to present the essential argument of this book in the Jefferson Memorial Lectures in 1981. For many helpful comments and criticisms I am indebted to my Yale colleagues in the faculty seminar on American Democratic Institutions, to the readers of the manuscript for the University of California Press, and to Joseph LaPalombara, Nelson Polsby, and Aaron Wildavsky. My debt to several generations of graduate students in my seminar on the government of economic enterprises, though less precise, is no less great. Research by Jo Beld Fraatz was of great help to me in writing Chapter 2. Finally, I appreciate the contributions of Amy Einsohn, who made useful suggestions and corrections as copyeditor, and Mary Renaud, who as staff editor guided the manuscript through the process of editing and publication.

Introduction

Within a generation or so after the Constitutional Convention, a rough consensus appears to have been reached among Americans—among white male citizens, at any rate—that a well-ordered society would require at least three things: political equality, political liberty, and economic liberty; that circumstances in the United States made it possible for Americans to attain these ends; and that, in fact, to a reasonably satisfactory degree these three ends had already been attained in America. Such was the state of mind that Alexis de Tocqueville encountered among Americans in 1831.

At the same time, however, some eminent and philosophically minded observers of the human condition believed that the three goals might very well conflict with one another, quite possibly, indeed, *must* conflict with one another. John Adams, Thomas Jefferson, and James Madison, together with many of Madison's fellow members of the American Constitutional Convention, were deeply concerned that political equality might conflict with political liberty. This possibility forms a major theme—in my view, *the* major theme—of Tocqueville's *Democracy in America*. Echoing an already ancient idea, in the pen-

ultimate chapter of his second volume Tocqueville asserts his belief that

> it is easier to establish an absolute and despotic government
> amongst a people in which the conditions of society are
> equal, than amongst any other; and I think that if such a
> government were once established amongst such a people,
> it would not only oppress men but would eventually strip
> each of them of several of the highest qualities of human-
> ity. Despotism therefore appears to me peculiarly to be
> dreaded in democratic ages. I should have loved freedom, I
> believe, at all times, but in the time in which we live I am
> ready to worship it.
>
> *(Tocqueville [1835] 1961, 2:385)*

   While Tocqueville was mainly concerned with the
threat that equality—political, social, and economic—
posed for *political* liberty and personal independence,
many of the Constitution's framers had been alarmed
by the prospect that democracy, political equality,
majority rule, and even political liberty itself would
endanger the rights of property owners to preserve
their property and use it as they chose. In this sense,
democracy was thought to menace *economic* liberty as
it was then commonly conceived—in particular, that
kind of liberty represented by the right to property.
Like the conflict between equality and political liberty, this potential conflict between democracy and
property was also part of a much older debate. In the
United States, the concern expressed at the Constitutional Convention has been frequently voiced ever
since.

In considering the threat posed by equality to liberty, Tocqueville, like Jefferson and the Framers before him, observed a society in which it was by no means unreasonable to expect, and hope, that male citizens would be approximately equal in their resources—property, knowledge, social standing, and so on—and consequently in their capacities for influencing political decisions. For they saw a country that was still overwhelmingly agrarian: seven of every ten persons gainfully employed were in agriculture, and the citizen body was predominantly composed of free farmers, or farmhands who aspired to become free farmers. What no one could fully foresee, though advocates of a republic constituted by free farmers sometimes expressed worrisome anticipations, was the way in which the agrarian society would be revolutionized by the development of the modern corporation as the main employer of most Americans, as the driving force of the economy and society. The older vision of a citizen body of free farmers among whom an equality of resources seemed altogether possible, perhaps even inevitable, no longer fitted that reality of the new economic order in which economic enterprises automatically generated inequalities among citizens: in wealth, income, social standing, education, knowledge, occupational prestige and authority, and many other resources. Had Tocqueville and his predecessors fully anticipated the shape of the economic order to come, they probably would have viewed the problem of equality and liberty in a different light. For if, in the older view, an equality among citizens might endanger liberty, in the new reality the liberty of corporate enterprises helped to create a body of citizens highly unequal in the resources they could bring to political life.

The question I want to confront, therefore, is whether it would be possible for Americans to construct a society that would more nearly achieve the values of democracy and political equality and at the same time preserve as much individual liberty as we now enjoy, and perhaps even more. Or is there an inescapable trade-off between liberty and equality, so that we can only enjoy the liberties we now possess by forgoing greater equality? Would therefore the price of greater equality necessarily be less liberty?

More concretely, I propose to explore the possibility of an alternative economic structure that would, I believe, help to strengthen political equality and democracy by reducing inequalities originating in the ownership and control of firms in a system like that we now possess—a system that for want of a better term I call *corporate capitalism*. The last three chapters describe an alternative, explain its justification, and examine some of its problems.

In examining this possibility I have deliberately narrowed the scope of our inquiry into the problem of freedom and equality: first by focusing on *political* equality, then by focusing on the consequences of owning and controlling enterprises. Important as it is, political equality—equality among citizens engaged in governing themselves by means of the democratic process—is not the only relevant form of equality that might serve as a standard for a good society. And owning and controlling firms is not the only source of undesirable inequalities among human beings, or even of political inequalities.

Yet narrowing the focus is, I believe, justified on several grounds. For one, the *general* problem of equality is so complex that perhaps we can deal with it well only by examining parts of it. As Douglas Rae concludes at the end of his masterly analysis of the meaning, kinds, and values of equality:

Equality is the simplest and most abstract of notions, yet the practises of the world are irremediably concrete and complex. How, imaginably, could the former govern the latter? It cannot. We are always confronted with more than one practical meaning for equality and equality itself cannot provide a basis for choosing among them. The question "Which equality?" will never be answered simply by insisting upon equality.

(Rae 1981, 150)

Moreover, of the various kinds of equality that might exist in a good society, political equality is surely one of the most crucial, not only as a means of self-protection but also as a necessary condition for many other important values, including one of the most fundamental of all human freedoms, the freedom to help determine, in cooperation with others, the laws and rules that one must obey. In a somewhat similar way, differences in ownership and control of enterprises, while certainly not at the origin of all forms of inequality, are deeply implicated in inequalities of many kinds: in esteem, respect, and status, in control over one's daily life, in income and wealth and all the opportunities associated with them, in life chances for adults and children alike. It seems to me scarcely open to doubt that a society with significantly greater equality in owning and controlling economic enterprises would produce profoundly greater equality than exists among Americans today.

Before considering whether an alternative to corporate capitalism might strengthen political equality without sacrificing liberty, we first need to search for a clearer understanding of the relationships between political equality, political liberty, and economic liberty. In my view these relationships have often been misconceived, or asserted in so general a fashion that we can scarcely judge the truth of statements about them. An enormously influential example of what I believe to be a mistaken view of these relationships is to be found in a very great work by a very great writer—Tocqueville himself, in *Democracy in America*. In the first chapter I examine this view, insofar at least as it can be teased out of Tocqueville's two volumes, and explain why I think his view is in some crucial respects misleading. In the second chapter I set out my conception of the relations between democracy, political equality, and economic liberty. The alternative discussed in the last three chapters may then be seen as an element in a system of liberties and equalities superior to what Americans now possess.

1

Is Equality Inimical to Liberty?

According to an old and widespread view, equality is a danger to liberty. But why and how, exactly, does equality threaten liberty? What kinds of "equality" and what kinds of "liberty"? And in order to judge the validity of answers to questions like these, what body of experience should we draw on?

An appropriate place to look for answers is Tocqueville's *Democracy in America*. For although what is immediately obvious to the reader is Tocqueville's fascination with equality and its effects, his central concern and his highest value is liberty. A fundamental theme running through both volumes is his fear that equality will crush liberty, and his search for a solution to the problem of how, if at all, they might be made to coexist.

However, because his argument and his answers are not always explicit, my interpretation seeks to make Tocqueville far more distinct and schematic

than he was or, I feel sure, would have wished to be.[1]
Although my treatment may do less than full justice
to Tocqueville, it may help us to grasp why equality
is so often seen as a threat to liberty, and to uncover
some of the problematic aspects of such a view.

Tocqueville's Argument

Let me summarize what I understand to be the essential premises of Tocqueville's argument in four sets
of propositions. *First*, throughout the civilized world
equality is increasing and inevitable. Because equality has nearly reached its natural limits among the
(white, male) citizens of the United States, America is
a testing ground for the world, and, not least, for
France. *Second*, liberty is a good of supreme importance, perhaps indeed a good greater than equality;
but the love of equality is stronger than the love of
liberty. While the advance of equality is sure, then,
the survival of liberty is more doubtful. *Third*, a necessary condition for liberty is the existence of strong
barriers to the exercise of power, for concentrated
power inherently spells the death of liberty. In the

1. Although Tocqueville was in my view a great political theorist, he was not the *kind* of theorist who deals explicitly with the
sorts of questions raised in the paragraph above. His theory is
often implicit, deeply embedded in its context, and highly qualified. The attempt to make his theory more explicit, less con-
textual, and less qualified, as I do here, is to attribute to him a
theory that he himself might have found unacceptable.

past, liberty has sometimes been protected against concentrated power by the existence of strong intermediate organizations standing between the individual and the state. However—and *fourth*—in a democratic country where political, social, and economic equality prevail, and all barriers to the unlimited exercise of power by the majority are removed, the majority has an opportunity to rule despotically: "The very essence of democratic government consists in the absolute sovereignty of the majority; for there is nothing in democratic states which is capable of resisting it (Tocqueville [1835] 1961, 1:298)." Taken together, these four assumptions constitute strong grounds for Tocqueville's fear that in a democratic society polity equality will invite the destruction of liberty. Indeed, the more democratic a people are, it would seem, the greater the danger to liberty.

In effect, then, Tocqueville poses a crucial dilemma. For although equality is clearly a *necessary* condition for democracy, it may not be a necessary condition for liberty; and equality is definitely not a sufficient condition. On the contrary, because equality facilitates majority despotism, it threatens liberty. If a necessary condition for democracy is a standing danger to liberty, must we therefore choose between democracy and liberty? Not necessarily, Tocqueville assures us, and offers a solution that might enable a people such as he believed the Americans to be to escape the dilemma of equality versus liberty. Before discussing his solution, however, we need a clearer understanding of the problem itself.

Equality.   Tocqueville emphasizes two closely related kinds of equality, which I am going to call *equality in political resources* and *equality of power*. As to
resources, he notes the relative equality among Americans in their capacities for physical resistance and coercion, such as firearms, military organization, and
police; in their legal authority over the state as citizens; in their knowledge; and in their wealth, income,
and social standing. Adopting an assumption common in political theory since the classical Greek era,
he believes that a rough equality in the distribution of
resources like these facilitates a rough equality in the
distribution of power, or more specifically, in control
over the government (or governments) of the state.
The political consequences of the extraordinary equality of social condition he finds among Americans are,
he tells us,

easily deducible. It is impossible to believe that equality
will not eventually find its way into the political world as it
does everywhere else. To conceive of men remaining for-
ever unequal upon a single point, yet equal on all others, is
impossible; they must come in the end to be equal upon all.

But ever mindful of the precarious position of liberty
in a world of equals, Tocqueville warns that "equality
in the political world" may be established in either of
two ways:

Every citizen must be put in possession of his rights, or
rights must be granted to no one.
From the same social position, then, nations may derive

one or the other of two great political results; these results are extremely different from one another, but they may both proceed from the same cause.

Having escaped the worse alternative, "the dominion of absolute power," Americans have so far managed to establish and maintain the sovereignty of the people (1:46–47). Yet it follows from Tocqueville's assumptions that among Americans the defense of liberty is arrayed against the preponderant and menacing forces of a majority of people who are remarkable in the degree to which they approach an absolute equality of resources and power.

To grasp Tocqueville's argument in its historical context, we need to note two important qualifications. First, although the United States was the only country—in world history, the first nation—that could then be called a democracy, it fell well short of our present inclusionary standards of democracy because a majority of the adult population—women, slaves, and most nonwhites—were denied political rights. Tocqueville's democracy in America was, at most, a democracy among American white males. Second, in describing the "unlimited power of the majority in the United States, and its consequences" what he had in mind was not so much the federal government as the individual state governments. For in his view the states were "in reality the authorities which direct society in America" (1:298). The principal source of his fear was not, then, the government of the American republic; it was, as he said, the "Governments of the American republics" (1:317). In fact,

by providing for separation of powers, federalism,
and a bill of rights, the American federal constitution
was among the "causes which mitigate the tyranny of
the majority" and "tend to maintain the Democratic
republic in the United States" (1:319–92). I shall return to this point, but I do not think the significance
of his argument is greatly diminished by his having
located the problem in the state governments.

Liberty.   Precisely how, we might ask, does political
equality, reinforced by an equality in political resources, endanger liberty? Tocqueville offers several
possibilities. One is mob rule or intimidation, which
is made all the more powerful because public opinion
stands behind the mob; for since no jury will convict
the wrongdoers, the injured have no effective re-
course to the protection of the laws (1:306–7, n.1). It
is true that Americans have often taken the law into
their own hands, and it was Americans, after all, who
coined the oxymoron "lynch law." Yet the century
and a half that separates us from Tocqueville shows
that while mob action is (or, one hopes, was) an American disease, it has not been common in democratic
countries. Indeed, in some countries that have become democratic since Tocqueville's time we find an
unusual deference to law. A propensity for mob rule
may have less to do with equality, then, than with
cultural and social variations among—and within—
countries. Although I do not mean to minimize the
importance of sporadic mob rule in American life, it
is not a general characteristic of democratic countries.

Tocqueville discerned a second danger, however, in the power of a majority in a society of equals to dominate public opinion itself by weakening potential deviance from majority views. A community of equals, in Tocqueville's view, would show a natural tendency toward conformity (1:309–16; 2:8–13). This propensity is perhaps the most serious and alarming defect that he ascribes to democracy in America, one possibly inherent in democracy itself. However, though he identified a problem of great importance, the effects of prevailing opinions on individual views are so complex and elusive that a satisfactory treatment would require a far more extensive theoretical and empirical inquiry than I wish to undertake here.

Two other dangers seem to me more directly relevant to the issue of equality versus liberty in democratic orders: the danger that the majority will oppress minorities through strictly legal processes, and the possibility that democratic societies will bring about a mass-based despotism which, while snuffing out all liberties, nonetheless ministers to the wants of the people and wins their support.

Majority Tyranny Through Law

The rights of every people are confined within the limits of what is just. . . . A majority taken collectively may be regarded as a being whose opinions, and most frequently whose interests, are opposed to those of another being, which is styled a minority. If it be admitted that a man,

possessing absolute power, may misuse that power by
wronging his adversaries, why should a majority not be li-
able to the same approach?

(1 : 304)

In asserting that in a democracy a majority and
its representatives may act legally, and yet unjustly,
Tocqueville was stating a commonplace of political
thought. To suggest this possibility, however, is only
to pose a problem—or rather a set of problems.

Theoretical problems.   To begin with, in order to judge
when a majority misuses its powers by wronging its
adversaries (to paraphrase Tocqueville), obviously we
need some criteria. What should these criteria be?
In the United States, opponents of important legal
changes, from the abolition of slavery to the imposi-
tion of an income tax and social security, have regularly denounced the proposed changes as abuses of
majority power, or worse, as outright cases of majority tyranny. Are we to say, then, that whenever the
interests of a minority are opposed to those of a majority, a majority necessarily misuses its power simply because it acts to secure its own interests? But
such an accusation is clearly absurd; for surely one of
the objectives of the democratic process is to permit a
majority to protect its interests. As Tocqueville himself says, "The moral power of the majority is founded
upon . . . [the principle] . . . that the interests of the
many are to be preferred to those of the few" (1 : 300).
    Evidently, then, we need to identify a subset of in-
stances of majority rule in which a majority, in using

its superior power, acts *unjustly* (and perhaps tyrannically) toward a minority. But what criteria should we use to distinguish injustice from a straightforward and entirely proper use of majority power? Is every instance of majority injustice also an instance of majority tyranny, or instead is majority tyranny, in turn, a special case of majority injustice?

In choosing criteria by which to decide whether a given law is unjust or even tyrannical (assuming that the first need not imply the second), we might easily construe either term so broadly that democracy or majority rule virtually become illegitimate by definition. For example, to define as unjust, or as tyrannical, any law that deprives some person of an existing legal right or injures a person's interests in any way whatsoever is obviously too broad. Since most laws alter existing legal rights and injure someone's interests in some way, so broad a definition would make any change in existing laws unjust, which is absurd.

Suppose we were to define tyranny a little more narrowly as the destruction of anyone's "*essential* interests." As James Fishkin has shown, on a reasonable interpretation of "essential interests," it would follow that in some situations any policy is bound to lead to *either* injustice *or* tyranny. For example, if child labor is in some circumstances unjust; and if it is an essential interest of employers to hire children; and if existing laws protect the legal right of employers to hire children: then either child labor cannot be legally forbidden, which would be unjust, or by forbidding it a government must necessarily act tyrannically. Nor can this kind of problem be solved by replacing the majority principle with any alternative numerical requirement. Take one possibility: A requirement of unanimity would no doubt prevent majority "tyranny"; but it would do so by giving every employer a veto on policy, and so would enable a single employer to prevent passage of a law barring the injustice of child labor (Fishkin 1979, 19ff.). Any requirement between a simple majority and unanimity creates the same issue.

We run the opposite risk, however, by defining injustice or tyranny so narrowly that they virtually vanish by definition.[2] Suppose, for example, we were to specify that any outcome of a desirable process for making decisions by definition produces a just decision. Following this definition, we would need only to believe that the democratic process is desirable in order to conclude that decisions made by means of a democratic process could never be unjust. But this conclusion is surely unacceptable. To be sure, procedural justice is extremely important; often it may be the only form of justice that can be assured. Yet we are entitled to ask in any particular case whether the outcome of a desirable procedure is itself just. Trial by one's peers may be a just procedure and may even be superior, in major criminal cases, to any alternative procedure. But we may reasonably doubt whether a jury's verdict is always substantively just. Likewise, even if you believe that the democratic process is pro-

2. I now think I came perilously close to doing so in *A Preface to Democratic Theory* (1956, 22–24) and find that treatment unsatisfactory.

cedurally just, you could reasonably assert that a decision by a wholly democratic process might sometimes produce substantive injustice.

Thus unless we possess satisfactory criteria for distinguishing instances of injustice and tyranny from ordinary use of the democratic process, it is impossible to judge the occurrence, frequency, and seriousness of the problem with which Tocqueville is concerned: majority abuse of power, majority injustice to minorities, and majority tyranny. Unfortunately, the two volumes of *Democracy in America* furnish so meagre a response to the kinds of questions I have just suggested that we must turn elsewhere for answers.[3]

Even if we were able to establish satisfactory criteria for identifying instances of majority injustice and majority tyranny, a crucial problem would remain. With what should we compare the performance of democratic regimes? Suppose it were shown that by acceptable criteria democracies sometimes act unjustly—even tyrannically. But suppose it were also shown that by the same criteria *all* regimes sometimes act unjustly and tyrannically? Where would that leave us? Fishkin has demonstrated that even on a quite restricted definition of tyranny—one much narrower than most discussions of majority tyranny assume—no theoretical guarantees against tyranny ap-

3. Answers might perhaps be teased out of Tocqueville's complete *oeuvre* though I am somewhat doubtful. For example, *The Old Regime and the French Revolution* is not very helpful on this point.

pear to exist. Neither procedural requirements, such as majority rule or its various modifications all the way to unanimity, nor absolute rights, nor "structural principles" like John Rawls's two principles of fairness can be counted on to prevent tyranny (Fishkin 1979).

It is of course easy to show that on any definition that is not simply vacuous, a majority *might* harm the interests of a minority, *might* act unjustly, *might* indeed act tyrannically. But if every alternative kind of regime would also permit injustice and tyranny, then it can hardly be counted as a unique defect of democracy or the majority principle that they do not totally foreclose these possible wrongs. Surely a question to ask is whether democracy is more prone to this kind of wrongdoing than any of the alternatives to it. Or is it, in practice, perhaps a good deal less prone?

To answer these questions, however, we need to distinguish two issues often confounded in discussions of liberty versus equality. First, we must ask ourselves whether any alternative kind of *regime*—that is, some kind of nondemocratic regime—would ensure greater liberty to its people. Second, even if democratic regimes are shown to be superior to nondemocratic regimes in ensuring liberty among their people, do they nonetheless frequently injure fundamental rights and liberties? If so, to what extent does this impairment of liberty result from equality and majority rule?

Comparison with nondemocratic regimes. There can really be no doubt that by Tocqueville's standards a more extensive liberty is secured in democratic than in nondemocratic regimes. To be sure, democracy might look inferior if the actual performance of some actual democratic regime were compared with the ideal performance of a hypothetical nondemocratic regime. Conversely, however, a comparison between the ideal performance of an ideal democratic regime and the actual performance of any actual nondemocratic regime would prove enormously to the advantage of the democratic ideal. But it is hard to know what to make of comparisons like these. If we were to consider only ideal regimes, then democracy would, on Tocqueville's terms, come out looking better: for no ideal regime except democracy can promise so wide a range of political liberties extended to so many of its people. What is more, no ideal regime except democracy can even promise to secure for most adults one of the most fundamental forms of liberty—the liberty of participating fully in the process of governing oneself.

Suppose then we were to consider only actual regimes. In his own time Tocqueville had no more to go on than the brief American experience arrayed against the background of all historical regimes. But previous regimes included only a few that by reasonable standards, including Tocqueville's, could be called democratic. Even so, he offered his readers no systematic comparisons. Yet I do not think he would have contested a claim that in 1832, despite slavery, harsh violence against the native Indian population, and the legal subjection of women, a higher proportion of Americans enjoyed a greater degree of politi-

cal freedom and civil liberty than had the people of
any regime then existing, or any earlier regime, with
the possible exceptions of classical Athens and the
Roman Republic. In the contemporary world political rights and liberties are much more secure in democratic than in nondemocratic countries.

It should not be altogether surprising to discover
that in democratic countries people possess a more
extensive range of political liberties than in nondemocratic countries, for the democratic process is inextric-
ably tied to certain rights and liberties. Consequently,
a hard-nosed methodologist might pronounce the relation "spurious," for some of the indicators used to
rank countries according to the extensiveness of political rights and civil liberties would also be used to
classify countries as democratic. Nonetheless, the in-
extricable connection between the democratic process
and rights and liberties does bear on Tocqueville's
concerns about democracy. The relation is "spurious"
only in a certain methodological sense. In distinguishing among political systems in the world of actual nations, it is highly significant.

Violations of basic liberties.   The conclusion that political and civil liberties are greater, perhaps much greater,
under democratic regimes than under nondemocratic
regimes may strike many readers as akin to the statement that people who are not in prison generally enjoy more freedom than people who are. A favorable
comparison of liberty under democratic and nondemocratic regimes hardly seems sufficient to meet
head-on the problem of majority tyranny posed by

Tocqueville. For there is no convincing reason for thinking that we have to settle for democratic regimes that merely scrape by, performing satisfactorily only by comparison with regimes of an inferior type. Is there not some standard against which we could compare the performance of a democracy? If so, and if democracies fall short of that standard, at least some of the time, how much of the failure is attributable to equality and the power of majorities?

These are tricky questions, extraordinarily difficult to answer, and once again Tocqueville gives us almost no help. But we can proceed by first specifying some rights that we might reasonably agree are in some sense fundamental, possibly even entitled to be considered morally "inalienable."[4] We can then examine whether and how much these fundamental rights are, or have been, threatened by democratic governments. Two bodies of rights are particularly germane to the concerns of Tocqueville, the Framers of the American Constitution, and no doubt many others who fear majority tyranny: economic rights, particularly property rights, and political rights. I shall consider economic rights in the next chapter and turn now to political rights. In a moment I shall suggest a theoretical basis for certain fundamental political rights. Meanwhile, we can probably agree that fundamental political rights would include the right to vote, to free

4. *Inalienable* in the sense that they cannot properly be surrendered, whether voluntarily or involuntarily. Although standard English usage in Jefferson's time was *unalienable*, he and the Declaration gave us *inalienable* (Wills 1978, 370). I stick with Jefferson's usage here.

speech, to free inquiry; the right to seek and hold
public office, and to free, fair, and moderately frequent elections; and the right to form political associations, including political parties. Let us call these *primary political rights.*

To what extent do equality and democracy endanger primary political rights?

As I have already remarked, Tocqueville was necessarily limited to scarcely two generations of experience in a single country. We have the advantage not
only of an additional 150 years but also the experience
of a much larger number of countries—roughly three
dozen in which democratic institutions, by present-
day standards, have existed for a generation or longer.
Unfortunately, no adequate comparative history of
political rights in democratic countries since Tocqueville's time has ever been undertaken. However, the
historical record seems to show a fairly steady strengthening and expansion of primary political rights in
democratic countries. In all democratic countries the
suffrage, for example, is much broader today than it
was in the United States in 1830. Again, while in 1830
secrecy in voting was a rarity, today it is standard
and, on the whole, effectively protected. In addition,
the rights of oppositions have been greatly expanded.
In many democratic countries the spectrum of legal
parties participating in elections runs from a revolutionary (though not systematically violent) left to a
right that may espouse antidemocratic ideas. The
spectrum of legally protected publications is, if any-

thing, even broader. Freedom of inquiry and expression are, by and large, extremely well protected in democratic countries—probably far better protected than they have ever been.

In several important respects the United States has been a deviant case. Here a racial minority suffered a deprivation of fundamental political and human rights unequaled in any other democratic country both in the number of persons victimized and in the severity of the deprivations. This deviance from democratic standards is at least partly explained by the fact that no other democratic country has contained as large a minority of inhabitants who acquired nominal citizenship only after a long period of slavery, were also racially distinct, and as a consequence were segregated into a distinct and subordinate caste. However that may be, except for the brief interlude of Reconstruction the political rights of blacks have been effectively protected in most of the South only since the mid 1960s. Even in this most extreme of cases, however, the historical thrust, glacial though it has been, is toward an expansion, not a contraction, of political rights.

Americans may also be unique in the frequency and savagery with which our fears of deviance from American orthodoxies erupt periodically into paranoidal witch-hunts that infringe the rights of political minorities, particularly on the left (Hofstadter 1965). Yet the larger background of American history and the experiences of other democratic countries warrants the conclusion that democracies tend toward an expansion, not a contraction, of the scope and effectiveness of legal protections for primary political rights. Deprivations and denials of rights occurring in the early life of democratic regimes tend to be reduced or even eradicated, not increased.

Since Tocqueville is silent on this point, I cannot be altogether sure how this conclusion joins with his assumptions. However, the historical evidence to date seems to me to provide scant support for the view that the destruction of fundamental political rights by means of laws passed according to democratic procedures is a salient characteristic of democratic countries. As in comparison with all other regimes, historical and contemporary, modern democracies are, by comparison with their own earlier experience, unique in the scope of the political rights protected by law and the proportion of the adult population who may effectively exercise those rights.

Depending on how one views the theoretical relation between democracy and rights, this conclusion might seem either obvious or surprising. For the nature of political rights in a democratic order can be viewed from several different and sometimes conflicting perspectives. Although these perspectives might yield essentially the same body of rights, they may have quite different implications for the way in which one thinks about the relation between democracy and rights. One perspective—let me call it the *theory of prior rights*—is familiar to Americans and indirectly has been incorporated in much of our constitutional thought. In the theory of prior rights, fundamental rights (including political rights) are in some sense anterior to democracy. They possess a moral exis-

tence, a standing, an ontological basis, if you will, altogether independent of democracy and democratic
processes. In this view certain fundamental rights are
not only anterior to democracy but superior to it.
They serve as limits on what can be done, properly at
least, by means of democratic processes. In the theory
of prior rights, then, fundamental political rights are
seen as rights a citizen is entitled to exercise, if need
be, *against* the democratic process. The liberty they
make possible is potentially threatened *by* the democratic process. It follows that to preserve fundamental
political rights and liberties a people must protect
them from infringement by, among other things, the
citizen body acting through the democratic process
itself.

An alternative way of thinking about fundamental
political rights is more consistent with democratic
ideas. This is to understand fundamental political
rights as comprising all the rights *necessary to* the democratic process. In this perspective, the right to self-
government through the democratic process is itself
one of the most fundamental rights that a person can
possess. Indeed, if any rights can be said to be inalienable, surely this must be among them. Consequently,
any infringement of the right to self-government
must necessarily violate a fundamental, inalienable
right. But if people are entitled to govern themselves,
then citizens are also entitled to all the rights that are
necessary in order for them to govern themselves—
that is, all the rights that are essential to the democratic process. On this reasoning, a set of basic political rights can be derived from one of the most

fundamental of all the rights to which human beings
are entitled—the right of self-government.

It can be shown, I believe, that the rights necessary
to the democratic process include *all* the political
rights I described earlier—rights that, when viewed
from the more familiar perspective of the prior rights
theory, would be regarded as superior to and threatened by democracy.

The tyranny that many people, including Tocqueville, seem to fear from democracy would come about
if a majority, though acting through the democratic
process in a perfectly legal way, were to diminish the
fundamental rights of any person subject to the laws.
I do not think this fear is unreasonable; but notice
how the way of looking at primary political rights I
have just suggested shifts the theoretical nature of the
problem.

To begin with, we no longer confront a straightforward conflict between liberty on the one side and
equality or democracy on the other. For if democracy
itself is a fundamental right, then a person's fundamental liberty consists, in part, of the opportunity to
exercise that right. If citizens in a majority, being entitled to liberty and to democratic rights, should in
exercising their rights restrict the rights and liberties
of a minority, a conflict exists between the rights and
liberties of some, who constitute a majority, and the
rights and liberties of others, who are a minority. Insofar as equality is at issue, it is an equal claim to the
rights entailed in a system of fundamental rights and
liberties—a kind of equality that few people con-

cerned with Tocqueville's problem would be likely to challenge.

Moreover, if a majority were to deprive a minority, or even itself, of any of its primary political rights, then in doing so it would also, precisely to that extent, destroy the democratic process. If they did so, and their decision were not simply a mistake, then it would necessarily be true that they were not, to that extent, committed to the democratic process itself. Conversely, if a people were committed to the democratic process, they would not, except by mistake, infringe on the primary political rights of any citizens.

Because the problem has been a source of confusion in democratic theory, it is useful to distinguish two cases: a majority versus the rights of a minority, and a majority versus democracy itself.

1. *Majority versus minority.* Is a majority entitled to use its primary political rights to deprive a minority of *its* primary political rights? The answer is sometimes presented as a paradox: If a majority cannot do so, then in effect it is deprived of its own rights; but if it can do so, then it deprives the minority of its rights. Thus no solution can be both democratic and just. But the dilemma seems to me spurious.

Of course, a majority might have the *power* or strength to deprive a minority of its political rights, though in practice I would guess that more often it is a powerful minority that strips a majority of its political rights rather than the other way round. In any event, judgments like these entail an empirical analysis of the dynamics of power, and arguably a full discussion of rights is incomplete without it. But a purely empirical analysis of these tendencies is not at the moment the issue here. The question is whether a majority may *rightly* use its primary political rights to deprive a minority of its primary political rights.

The answer is clearly no. To put it another way, logically it cannot be true that a given aggregate of persons ought to govern themselves by democratic processes, and that a majority of those persons may properly strip a minority of their primary political rights. For by doing so, the majority denies the minority the rights necessary to the democratic process; in effect therefore the majority affirms that this aggregate of persons ought not to govern themselves by democratic processes. One cannot have it both ways.

2. *A majority versus democracy*. May not a demos, the collectivity of citizens, decide that it simply doesn't want to be governed by democratic processes? May a people not use the democratic process to replace democracy with a nondemocratic regime? Again, one meets an alleged paradox: Either a people does not have the right, in which case it is unable to govern itself democratically, or it does have the right, in which case it may democratically choose to be governed by a dictator. In either case, the democratic process is bound to lose.

Empirically, it is obviously true that a demos might choose to employ democratic processes to destroy those processes. If democratic processes exist, they can hardly constitute an insuperable barrier to a majority doing so. This empirical possibility is relevant in assessing how desirable that process is, whether generally or among a particular people. If in the history of democratic trial and error various peoples had frequently voted out democracy, one might pessimistically conclude that democratic regimes are so prone to self-destruction that the democratic idea is radically flawed. The immediate question, however, is not primarily empirical in aim but, once again, whether a demos may *rightfully* do what it clearly *can* do, or, to use a different terminology, whether it has the authority to do what it has the power to do. Posed this way, the argument that a demos may rightfully employ the democratic process in order to destroy democracy is as badly conceived as the previous argument that a majority may rightfully deprive a minority of its rights. Since the two arguments are in essence the same, the dilemma is as spurious in the one case as in the other. If it is desirable that a people should govern itself democratically, then it cannot be desirable that it be governed undemocratically. If people believe that democracy is desirable and justified, logically they cannot simultaneously believe that it is undesirable, and thereby justify the destruction of the democratic process.

Thus, since primary political rights are necessary to the democratic process, a people committed to the democratic process would be bound (logically) to uphold these rights. Conversely, if they were knowingly to infringe on these rights they would thereby declare their rejection of the democratic process. If we interpret Tocqueville as fearing that majority despotism would arise among a people as committed to the democratic process as he portrayed the Americans to be, then his fear reflected a theoretical mistake about the relation between fundamental political rights and the democratic process.

These theoretical considerations may appear to do no more than provide feeble, entirely formal barriers to majority tyranny. In practice, however, they can develop into the strongest protection that rights can have. For the democratic process is unlikely to be preserved unless the people of a country preponderantly believe that it is desirable, and unless this belief comes to be embedded in the habits, practices, and culture of that people. Despite the two different ways of looking at primary rights, the logic of democracy is not arcane. The relation between the democratic process and certain primary political rights is not so abstract as to lie beyond the reach of practical reason and common sense. Thinking about the requirements of their political system, a democratic people, its leaders, its intellectuals, and its jurists would see the practical need for primary political rights and would develop protections for them. As a result, among a people generally democratic in their commitments, a belief in the desirability of primary political rights might well become interwoven with their belief in democracy itself. Thus in a stable democracy a commitment to the protection of all the primary political rights would become an essential element of the political culture, particularly as that culture was transmitted by persons bearing a special responsibility for the interpretation and enforcement of rights—as jurists, for example, do.

At this point anyone familiar with *Democracy in America* may well wonder whether our theoretical route has not after all led us straight back to Tocqueville. For every reader of those two volumes will recall his strong emphasis on the importance of customs, habits, and mores for maintaining democracy and a balance between liberty and equality.

Before examining that proposition, however, we need to consider another way by which the dynamics of equality might, in Tocqueville's view, turn democracy into a new species of oppression.

Mass-based Despotism

The argument of the previous section does not entirely dispose of the possibility that democracy might be a natural breeding ground for the evolution of some kind of mass-based despotism. Is it not possible that only a few democratic countries, like the survivors of a highly lethal disease, have managed to develop a political culture containing sufficient resistance to the dangers of equality so as to ensure the survival of both political liberty and democracy? If so, in countries less fortunate than the survivors, the dynamics of equality may already have caused democracy to collapse. Such countries would be the casualties of a historical process by which democracy destroys itself. Even in countries now democratic, which still preserve all the primary political rights necessary to the democratic process and so look outwardly healthy, the effects of equality may already be working their fatal course through the society, like some incurable disease. Is the coexistence of democracy, equality, and primary political rights often, perhaps typically, no more than a transitional state between the birth of a new democratic order and its transformation into a mass-based despotism?

After completing the first volume of *Democracy in America*, Tocqueville seems to have been drawn more and more to an idea roughly along these lines. "A more accurate examination of the subject, and five years of further meditations," he wrote as he approached the end of his second volume, "have not diminished my apprehensions, but they have changed the object of them" (2:378). In one of the most haunting and evocative passages in all political writing, he then forecasts a wholly new form of despotism to be feared in democratic countries.

I think then that the species of oppression by which democratic nations are menaced is unlike anything which ever before existed in the world: our contemporaries will find no prototype of it in their memories. I am trying myself to choose an expression which will accurately convey the whole of the idea I have formed of it, but in vain; the old words despotism and tyranny are inappropriate: the thing itself is new; and since I cannot name it, I must attempt to define it.

I seek to trace the novel features under which despotism may appear in the world. The first thing that strikes the observation is an innumerable multitude of men all equal and alike, incessantly endeavoring to procure the petty and paltry pleasures with which they glut their lives. Each of them, living apart, is as a stranger to the fate of all the rest,—his children and his private friends constitute to him the whole of mankind; as for the rest of his fellow-citizens, he is close to them, but he sees them not,—he touches them, but he feels them not; he exists but in himself and for himself alone; and if his kindred still remain to him, he may be said at any rate to have lost his country.

Above this race of men stands an immense and tutelary power, which takes upon itself alone to secure their gratifications, and to watch over their fate. That power is absolute, minute, regular, provident, and mild. It would be like the authority of a parent, if, like that authority, its object was to prepare men for manhood; but it seeks on the contrary to keep them in perpetual childhood: it is well content that people should rejoice, provided they think of nothing but rejoicing. For their happiness such a government willingly labors, but it chooses to be the sole agent and the only arbiter of that happiness: it provides for their security, foresees and supplies their necessities, facilitates their pleasures, manages their principal concerns, directs their industry, regulates the descent of property, and subdivides their inheritances—what remains, but to spare them all the care of thinking and all the trouble of living?

Thus it every day renders the exercise of the free agency of man less useful and less frequent; it circumscribes the will within a narrower range, and gradually robs a man of all the uses of himself. The principle of equality has prepared men for these things: it has predisposed men to endure them, and oftentimes to look on them as benefits.

After having thus successively taken each member of the community in its powerful grasp, and fashioned them at will, the supreme power then extends its arm over the whole community. It covers the surface of society with a network of small complicated rules, minute and uniform, through which the most original minds and the most energetic characters cannot penetrate, to rise above the crowd. The will of man is not shattered, but softened, bent, and guided: men are seldom forced by it to act, but they are constantly restrained from acting: such a power does not destroy, but it prevents existence; it does not tyrannize, but it compresses, enervates, extinguishes, and stupefies a people, till each nation is reduced to be nothing better than a flock of timid and industrious animals, of which the government is the shepherd.

(2:380–81)

How are we to interpret this pessimistic prediction? It could be read as foreshadowing the growth of the welfare state, which has developed since Tocqueville's time in almost all democratic countries and in some, like Sweden, to an unusual degree. Some critics have contended that by increasing the dependence of citizens—legal, political, economic, and spiritual—on central officials of the state, the welfare state has correspondingly reduced their liberty and independence. But turning Tocqueville into a partisan in a now rather stale debate about the effects of the welfare state on political and other rights and liberties makes him a good deal less interesting and important than I believe him to be. Although once again we cannot be entirely sure what Tocqueville meant, an alternative interpretation seems to me more fruitful.

Let us suppose that in Tocqueville's view the equal-

ity he believed so characteristic of democratic countries would be peculiarly conducive, given enough
time to work its corrosive effects, to the growth of
widespread support for something vaguely like the
mass-based authoritarian regimes that have been such
an astounding feature of this century. Admittedly it
would be foolish to contend that he accurately foresaw the rise of these regimes, or, certainly, the extent
to which they employ overt violence, coercion, and
repression. He may have anticipated that the governments of these regimes would be more benign than
they are. But it is worth noting that to their supporters and apologists the power of many mass-based
modern authoritarian regimes may well seem, as
he forecasts, "absolute, minute, regular, provident,
and mild."

In summarizing Tocqueville's argument at the beginning of this chapter I said that he poses a dilemma:
democracy cannot exist without an exceptional degree
of social, economic, and political equality, yet that
very equality so essential to democracy also threatens
liberty. The dilemma reappears in the passage just
cited. Democracy requires equality, yet the degree of
equality necessary for democracy to exist also carries
with it a likelihood that a democratic regime will be
transformed into a historically unprecedented form of
despotism. We might recast Tocqueville's conjecture
along these lines: In democratic countries the equality
of condition that is necessary to democracy will, over
the long run, tend to create a highly atomized society
of isolated individuals and families, and to generate
support among a substantial majority of people for a

regime that undertakes to satisfy widespread popular desires for security, income, shelter, comfort, and the like, while at the same time drastically curtailing political rights and destroying the democratic process.

If this conjecture is correct, then because of the long-term consequences of equality and the necessary connection between equality and democracy, given enough time for the force of equality to work its effects, democratic systems will tend to be self-destructive in a special way. More specifically, among countries that have been democratic for a considerable period of time—let us say a generation or more—we should expect to find a significant number in which at least three observable changes take place: the society becomes atomized into isolated individuals; democracy is replaced by an authoritarian regime; and this change of regime is both supported by and comes about largely as a consequence of widespread popular support.

The breakdown of democratic institutions and their supersession by authoritarian regimes in Italy, Germany, Austria, and Spain from 1923 to 1936 seemed to many observers to validate Tocqueville's conjecture. Ortega's *Revolt of the Masses*, published in 1930 after the triumph of fascism in Italy but before democracy had been destroyed in Germany, Austria, and Spain, was often read as a farsighted anticipation of the collapse of mass-based democracy. During the next several decades the view was frequently advanced that the rise of mass democracy in the twentieth century threatened to bring about the destruction of political liberty and liberal democracy. Initially formulated mainly by scholars in exile, who themselves had witnessed the breakdown of democracy in their own land (notably Hannah Arendt, Emil Lederer, and Sigmund Neumann), the theory received its most systematic elaboration in 1959 by an American sociologist, William Kornhauser, in *The Politics of Mass Society*, a book that drew explicitly on Tocqueville.

The theory of mass democracy set forth by these writers has been subjected to intense and telling criticism. However, since the theory had mainly emphasized the atomization of society and the support that fascism supposedly derived from isolated, uprooted, and lonely individuals, it was on this feature of the theory that critics concentrated their fire. In a superb historical reconstruction of the social character of a single town in Germany in 1930, William S. Allen showed that Germans, far from being isolated, were involved in a dense network of associations. The fatal flaw, however, was that the organizations were polarized on class lines (Allen 1965). In a recent essay, Bernt Hagtvet has used a substantial body of evidence, including Allen's, to show with devastating effect that the destruction of the Weimar Republic did not come about as the theory of mass democracy had supposed (Hagtvet 1980). Because equivalent analysis is lacking for most other countries we cannot, of course, be certain that the atomization thesis is entirely wrong. But since the theory was in large part the creation of German exiles drawing mainly on German experience, if the theory is wrong about that crucial case, then it loses much of its plausibility.

Both the proponents and critics of the theory of

mass democracy have, as I said, concentrated mainly
on the supposed consequences of isolation for the rise
of authoritarianism. Yet while the evidence suggests
that this relationship is spurious, the movement from
political and social equality to support for authoritarian movements might nonetheless take something
like the path that Tocqueville charted. It is reasonable,
then, to consider whether the rise of mass-based authoritarian regimes in this century provides convincing evidence that, given sufficient time, modern
democracies tend to generate wide support for authoritarian movements, and thus to be transformed
into authoritarian regimes. A good test would be to
examine all known instances in which a modern democracy has been transformed into a dictatorship to
see whether the transformation fits the hypothesis. I
have been able to identify thirteen cases in this century in which a democratic regime (or in some cases a
quasi-democratic regime) has been transformed into a
dictatorship. These are: Argentina in 1930, Austria
1933–34, Brazil 1964, Chile 1973, Colombia 1949,
Germany 1933, Greece 1967, Italy 1923–25, Peru
1968, Portugal 1926, Spain 1936, Venezuela 1948, and
Uruguay 1973.[5]

What I find striking is how little support these cases
yield for the hypothesis, and indeed five aspects of the

5. My sources are Linz and Stepan (1978) and Morlino (1980,
94); to their lists I have added Uruguay, which curiously is omitted in both works. My list (like theirs) excludes postcolonial governments that were quickly transformed from parliamentary systems to dictatorships, particularly in Africa. Including these cases
would, however, only strengthen the argument that follows.

experiences of these countries seem to run sharply counter to the hypothesis.

1. With the single exception of Uruguay, at the time of democratic collapse all these countries had experienced less than twenty years under democratic institutions. It is much more reasonable to conclude that the breakdown of democracy resulted in part from the very novelty, fragility, and uncertain legitimacy of democratic institutions in these countries than from the long-run effects of social or political equality. In most of these countries democratic habits and practices had quite shallow roots. In Germany, a democratic regime had only recently replaced a non-democratic, indeed an authoritarian regime of a traditional kind. In some countries, political oppositions outside the closed circle of an oligarchy had only recently gained political rights. In others, like Italy and Chile, less than a generation had passed since the suffrage had been extended to most males. Using criteria of democracy like these, democratic institutions were only thirteen years old in Italy when Mussolini consolidated his power in 1925, fourteen years old in Argentina in 1930,[6] fourteen in Germany in 1933, fifteen in Austria in 1934, two in Spain in 1936, fourteen in Peru in 1968, and so on. Even in Chile, which was widely held to be one of a tiny handful of democratic

6. Although electoral reform took place in 1912, "the first elections with total participation of the citizenry were realized in 1916. . . . This date, 1916, can probably be taken as the beginning of mass democracy and the end of limited democracy . . ." (Germani 1969, 132).

countries in Latin America—a judgment in all other respects entirely correct—obstacles to registration had "resulted in a relatively small number of registered voters" until reforms in 1958 and 1962 greatly enlarged the suffrage (Gil 1966, 207).

The only exception I can find is Uruguay, where democratic practices seem to have been pretty much observed from the first part of this century until 1933 when the president, Gabriel Terra, carried out a coup d'etat. After nearly a decade of unconstitutional presidential rule by Terra and his successors, in 1942 Uruguay, as one writer put it, "now returned to the democratic way of life which Terra's action had interrupted" (Pendle 1963, 36). Thus Uruguay may be the *only* instance in which a relatively long-standing democratic system has been replaced by an internally imposed authoritarian regime.[7] By contrast, there are at least twenty-six countries in which democratic institutions have existed for more than twenty years, and in some cases, as we know, very much longer.[8]

7. Although Uruguay's democratic experience and breakdown have so far been little studied (see, however, Gillespie 1982), it appears that unlike the other countries listed above its democratic processes and institutions were deeply grounded in belief systems and political culture (Gonzalez 1982b, 27–28). The depth and persistence of its democratic culture provide grounds for expecting that a democratic system will reemerge in Uruguay (Gonzalez 1982a).

8. The countries are Australia, Austria, Belgium, Canada, Colombia, Costa Rica, Denmark, Finland, France, Iceland, Ireland, Israel, Italy, Jamaica, Japan, Luxembourg, Netherlands, New Zealand, Norway, Sweden, Switzerland, Trinidad and Tobago, United Kingdom, United States, Venezuela, and West Germany. I have omitted India because of the interlude in which Indira Gandhi suspended constitutional guarantees.

2. Moreover, in countries where a democratic regime was supplanted by authoritarianism not only did democratic institutions suffer from the fragility of recent implantation but the regime that broke down was, in some cases, at best only a partly democratized traditional oligarchy. Thus from a competitive oligarchy in 1910, by 1940 Colombia had developed into what has been described as an "oligarchical democracy" because, despite vigorous competition between the Conservatives and Liberals, electoral participation was ordinarily low (even by North American standards) and "fraud was always present, as was periodic coercion against the opposition" (Wilde 1978, 30–31, 44).[9] In Argentina, because of the persistence of a large number of unnaturalized immigrants, less than half the adult males had the right to vote; and because a large proportion of the working class were immigrants (around 60 percent in urban areas), much of the working class was effectively disfranchised.

3. In addition, in most of these countries a substantial proportion of the leadership and, so far as one can tell, the general population were hostile to egalitarianism, political equality, democratic ideas, and demo-

9. The difficulty of locating the Colombian system among either typical democracies or typical oligarchies is reflected in Wilde's careful qualification: "On balance, however, neither [fraud nor periodic coercion of oppositions] should be taken as reason to deny Colombia its place among historical 'democracies'" (p. 31). "With several qualifications, then, there was a kind of democracy established and operating in Colombia before November 1949" (p. 32). "When democracy was lost in 1949, much of Colombian politics did not change. The system remained oligarchical . . ." (p. 32). "The consociational character of Colombian democracy was clearly oligarchical" (p. 34).

cratic institutions. In Germany, it has been estimated that throughout the Weimar Republic only about 45 percent of the electorate favored a democratic order, while 35 percent supported a right-wing authoritarian order and another 10 percent a communist order. Thus democratic and antidemocratic support was about equal, while the remaining 10 percent were undecided between democracy and authoritarianism (Lepsius 1978, 38). It is hardly surprising that in Argentina a working class suffering from substantial disfranchisement and political discrimination should turn to Perón, as they were to do in overwhelming numbers. If the legitimacy of democracy was weak at the lower end of the Argentine social scale, it was even weaker at the top. The traditional oligarchy had adopted a standing rule that the "wrong" majority must never be allowed to win an election. When an electoral law of 1912 finally insured free and fair elections, the successors to the old oligarchy, the Conservatives, persisted in rejecting the legitimacy of majority rule. Dismayed in the 1920s by the seeming unwillingness of the Radicals, now the majority party, to share their control over government with them, the Conservatives supported a military coup (Botana 1977, 174–202; Smith 1978; O'Donnell 1978).

4. What is more, the transition from democracy or quasi democracy to authoritarianism has rarely if ever come about as a result of overwhelming public support making itself felt through democratic processes. Typically, prior to the transition the country is highly fragmented or, as in Germany, Austria, Colombia, and Chile, polarized into antagonistic camps. In vir-

tually every country the transition has been brought about not by means of democratic processes but through a violent seizure of power by professedly antidemocratic, authoritarian leaders who proceed swiftly and more or less openly to destroy democratic institutions. To be sure, Hitler legally became Reichschancellor in January 1933. But he quickly suspended constitutional civil rights, and the elections of March 1933 took place "in an atmosphere of public insecurity and terror for Communists and Socialists" (Lepsius, 73). Even so the Nazis won only 44 percent of the vote and needed the 8 percent conservative vote to provide them with a majority. Hitler thereupon rapidly interred the remains of the Weimar Republic.

In some countries—conceivably Germany may have been one—the authoritarian regime may have acquired the support of a majority of adults. With the unprecedented capacities for the manipulation and coercion of opinion available to a modern authoritarian state, that would hardly be surprising. But we cannot know for sure how often this was so, or when a majority, if one existed, might have decayed into a minority. In this respect, perhaps Argentina fits the hypothesis best. One of the keenest students of Argentine politics has described Perón as "undoubtedly a majoritarian dictator" during his rule from 1946 to 1955 (O'Donnell, 164). From the time Perón was overthrown, it was well understood among Argentine liberals and conservatives alike that if elections were held in which the Peronistas were allowed to participate, Perón would win at least a plurality of votes. Thus Perón's opponents confronted a dilemma:

should they hold free and fair elections, in which case Perón would win, or should they prevent him from winning by making it impossible for a plurality of voters to exercise a free choice in elections? Either way, democracy was sure to lose.

5. Peronism, however, did not grow out of an excess of equality but from strongly felt inequalities, political, social, and economic. The example of Perón, I think, makes the most telling point of all: the countries I have listed were not marked by a very high degree of social and economic equality.[10] In most, inequality was extreme, or was felt to be, and inequalities often helped to fragment or polarize the citizenry into hostile camps, to weaken confidence in democratic institutions, and to generate support for dictatorship, whether to enable the leaders of the *descamisados* to gain power or in order to stop them from doing so. If liberty was menaced in these countries, the threat came not from too much equality but from too little. The most fundamental factor that in Tocqueville's view might predispose a democratic people to destroy liberty—equality of condition—was absent.

Reprise

Was then Tocqueville fundamentally wrong? Not necessarily. For he did not contend that democratic

10. Once again, Uruguay was an exception. "Even now its income distribution is probably the most equalitarian in South America" (Gonzalez 1982b, 27).

equalities made the destruction of liberty inevitable. He argued only that they made it likely. But he also argued that under certain conditions, which he thought largely existed in the United States, equality might be reconciled with liberty. Of course he did not assume that American conditions and institutions could or even should be exactly duplicated in Europe or elsewhere. He did believe that stripped of their American peculiarities certain general factors could support democracy and liberty in other countries (1 : 384ff.).

He strongly emphasized four such factors.[11] One was a general diffusion of economic well-being or "physical prosperity." A century and a half after Tocqueville's insight, we indeed do find an extraordinarily strong correlation between economic well-being and democracy. Democratic institutions exist today exclusively in countries having high per capita gross national product, with only a few somewhat precarious exceptions like India, Greece, and Portugal. While such prosperity may be neither necessary nor sufficient for democracy, doubtless it greatly facilitates the emergence and survival of democratic institutions. Yet we must not misread the evidence.

11. I have drawn these from his discussions of associations: political (1, ch. 12); in civil life (2, bk. 2, chs. 5, 6, and 7); lawyers (1, ch. 16); other "Causes which mitigate the tyranny of the majority in the United States" (1, ch. 16); and "Principle causes which tend to maintain the Democratic Republic in the United States" (1, ch. 17). Evidently Tocqueville meant to distinguish the two sorts of causes in chapters 16 and 17 of volume 1. But since their general effect is to sustain both democracy and liberty, I have ignored the distinction.

Measured by the indicators of economic achievement most used in recent years, in comparison with contemporary industrial nations Americans in 1832 would be judged relatively poor. Democracy requires neither opulence nor the material standards that today prevail in advanced industrial countries. It requires instead a widespread sense of relative economic well-being, fairness, and opportunity, a condition derived not from absolute standards but from perceptions of relative advantage and deprivation (see also Dahl 1971, 62ff.).

Tocqueville also emphasizes the importance to democracy of a society in which power and social functions are decentralized among a large number of relatively independent associations, organizations, and groups. He stresses the vital role of independent newspapers (1, ch. 11), of lawyers as an independent profession (1, ch. 16), of political associations (1, ch. 12), and of associations in civil life, not only "commercial and manufacturing companies, but associations of a thousand other kinds—religious, moral, serious, futile, extensive or restricted, enormous or diminutive" (2:128). Tocqueville was one of the first to recognize the intimate relation between democratic institutions and a pluralistic society and polity. He was surely right. For despite substantial variations in particular patterns, in all modern democratic countries power is significantly decentralized among a variety of political, professional, economic, social, cultural, and religious organizations. To be sure, the existence of relatively independent organizations is not sufficient for democracy; but it is evidently necessary for democracy and liberty on a national scale (see also Dahl 1982). The development of a relatively independent church, a trade union movement, a farmers organization, and associations of intellectuals was not sufficient to make Poland a democracy. But these independent organizations were absolutely essential for whatever liberty and democracy the Poles enjoyed before the military takeover.

Third, Tocqueville called attention to the significance of constitutional decentralization in the United States—the separation of powers into three relatively independent centers, the territorial division of power between federal and state governments, the further decentralization to local units, and the decentralization of the judicial process through the Anglo-American system of trial by jury, by which he was strongly impressed. Tocqueville rightly foresaw that other democratic countries would not need to imitate the particularities of the American constitutional system. As it has turned out, in fact, no other existing democratic country has closely copied our system, whose constitution provides much more decentralized power among relatively independent institutions than most other countries have thought either necessary or desirable. Yet whatever a nation's formal constitutional theory, in every democratic country the judiciary is relatively independent of the executive and parliament; parliament retains at least a small measure of independence from the executive, though in some countries it has been slight at times; for better or worse, administrative agencies tend to be relatively independent of one another, of the executive, and of parliament; and some functions are reserved for local governments. As to the last, just as Tocqueville feared might happen, in France the Third, Fourth, and Fifth Republics all retained the stifling Napoleonic prefectural system with its taut central control over the *départements*. In a move that Tocqueville would no doubt have supported, not until 1981 did the French attempt to increase the autonomy of local governments so as to breathe more local democracy into a highly centralized system.

Yet much as he stressed the vital importance of the "laws"—or as we would say, the constitutional system—in uniting freedom with democracy and majority rule, Tocqueville attributed even greater significance to a fourth factor, one considerably more elusive than the others: the *manners* of a people, a term Tocqueville equated with the Latin *mores*. By *manners* he refers to "the various notions and opinions current among men, and to the mass of those ideas which constitute their character of mind" (1:354). On the relative importance of these manners, Tocqueville is succinct:

[If] they were to be classed in their proper order, I should say that the physical circumstances [of a country] are less efficient [in maintaining democracy] than the laws, and the laws very subordinate to the manners of the people. . . . So seriously do I insist upon this head, that if I have hitherto failed in making the reader feel the important influence which I attribute to the practical experience, the habits, the opinions, in short, to the manners of the Americans, upon the maintenance of their institutions, I have failed in the principal object of my work.

(1:383)

In attributing such an essential role to manners and mores, Tocqueville both echoed an older theme—sounded by Machiavelli in *The Discourses*, for example—and anticipated the importance attributed to "political culture" by many recent scholars. Like manners and mores, political culture is an elusive quality; probably in no area of comparative political analysis is good evidence so skimpy. The essential characteristics of a democratic culture, like those of a "democratic personality," remain uncertain and sharply debated. Yet scholars who attempt to grapple with the question "Why do democratic institutions exist in country X but not in country Y?" tend to agree sooner or later with Tocqueville, that neither prosperity nor a good constitutional system will ensure democracy among a people who lack the essential predispositions for it, attitudes that are transmitted and supported by the broader culture, belief systems, habits, manners, and mores. But a people who do possess such a culture might manage democratic institutions under one of many constitutional systems, and might do so through times of economic crisis that would bring about the collapse of democracy among a people with a less supportive political culture. To explain why democracy succumbed to dictatorship in Argentina in 1930, but in neither New Zealand nor Australia, requires more than a description of their economic circumstances, which were rather comparable, or an analysis of their constitutions.

Was Tocqueville fundamentally right after all? It is tempting to think so, for it is very likely true that in all countries where democratic institutions have survived along with the fundamental political liberties necessary to them, the four conditions suggested by Tocqueville have also been present and are sufficient to account for the reconciliation in these countries of democracy and liberty. If so, Tocqueville's implicit theory would appear to be vindicated.

Yet a troubling question remains. Even if Tocqueville's solution to the problem of liberty and equality is roughly right, is the danger as he formulated it a central problem in democratic countries? Tocqueville took equality as given and liberty as problematical. A grand historical process was bound to produce equality; but no such historical process ensured liberty. On the contrary, liberty was menaced by equality.

But can we really take equality as given? Or is it not also, like liberty, highly problematical? A combination of circumstances in the United States created in Tocqueville's time an equality of condition among white males that was then historically rare and probably unique in its scope. But that combination was more than merely unusual, and even in the United States it proved transitory. For the agrarian economy and society on which it was based underwent a revolutionary transformation into a new system of commercial and industrial capitalism that automatically generated vast inequalities of wealth, income, status, and power. These inequalities were in turn a result of liberty of a certain kind—liberty to accumulate unlimited economic resources and to organize economic activity into hierarchically governed enterprises.

The problem we face, and all modern democracies face, is therefore even more difficult than the one Tocqueville posed. For not only must we identify and create the conditions that reduce the possible adverse effects of equality on liberty but also we must strive to reduce the adverse effects on democracy and political equality that result when economic liberty produces great inequality in the distribution of resources and thus, directly and indirectly, of power.

Tocqueville advanced a reasonable solution to the problem he posed. But the problem of liberty and equality that we face is not precisely the same. The conditions for reconciling liberty and equality that he advanced are, I think, still necessary. But since equality is as problematic as liberty, the conditions he specified are no longer sufficient. The question we confront is whether we can create conditions as supportive of liberty as those Tocqueville thought Americans, and perhaps other nations, could provide, and as conducive to equality as he believed American society to be at a historical moment that is irreversibly behind us.

2

Democracy, Political Equality, and Economic Liberty

Among people who value freedom the fact that modern democracy has on the whole done well by political liberty should be an occasion for at least restrained rejoicing, perhaps meriting the two cheers for democracy that E. M. Forster offered after World War II, during which the future of democracy had been in grave doubt. To say that democratic institutions and the political rights they require have shown a certain capacity for survival is not to argue, however, that political equality is alive and well in the United States. As I suggested in the previous chapter, if, as Tocqueville thought, liberty is problematical even in democratic countries, so too is equality, which he mistakenly believed to be inevitable.

Why democratic institutions and a fair degree of political liberty have managed to survive in several dozen countries despite sizable differences among citizens in resources and opportunities, and despite recurrent predictions to the contrary, is a complex question that I do not intend to explore here. Among other reasons, it is worth mentioning that inequalities in democratic countries come in many varieties; the advantages and disadvantages of different varieties are not all concentrated in the same individuals, strata, or classes; given the political and legal structures of democratic countries, not all inequalities are readily convertible, if at all, into political inequality; and the advantages of superior resources often suffer from diminishing returns in political life. Though David Rockefeller is undoubtedly very much wealthier than Tip O'Neill, and though Paul Newman is infinitely more popular, neither would be so foolish as to suppose that he could obtain the congressman's support for any legislation he happened to favor.

Nonetheless, the existence of sizable inequalities in political resources among the citizens of a democratic country should be disturbing to anyone who places a high value on political equality. Such an undesirable state of affairs would be acceptable only if no feasible alternative could be found. Historical experience shows, however, that inequalities commonly thought to be ineradicable have often been dramatically reduced even if not totally abolished. For example, during the century following the American Civil War one of the greatest sources of political inequality among Americans was race. During most of that time a delicate balance of mutually advantageous political coalitions, combined with widespread attitudes among whites, effectively precluded action to eliminate this critical inequality. But by the 1960s a majority of Americans had come to accept the view that fundamental rights should be protected without regard to race, and the traditional political coalitions had become unstable; civil rights legislation was finally passed by Congress and vigorously enforced by the executive branch. What to generations of Americans had appeared to be an unchangeable system of political, social, and economic inequality was transformed through public policies, and the political rights of southern blacks were at last effectively protected. Once their political rights were guaranteed, blacks began to vote on a par with whites—an outcome that had been all but inconceivable a generation before.

But of course many sources of political inequality remain in the United States (and elsewhere), including race. The extent to which American citizens can or should become political equals partly depends on the extent to which the various remaining causes of political inequality can, and should, be reduced. Although some causes, such as individual differences in political interest, can be reduced, they will probably never be eliminated, because reducing individual differences beyond some point would turn out to be excessively costly to other values.

What about the ownership and control of economic enterprises as a source of political inequality? Ownership and control of firms affects political inequality in two ways that are closely related but rather different. First, ownership and control contribute to the creation of great differences among citizens in wealth, income, status, skills, information, control over information and propaganda, access to political leaders, and, on the average, predictable life chances, not only for mature adults but also for the unborn, infants, and children. After all due qualifications have been made, differences like these help in turn to generate significant inequalities among citizens in their capacities and opportunities for participating as political equals in *governing the state*.

Second, and even more obvious, with very few exceptions the internal governments of economic enterprises are flatly undemocratic both de jure and de facto. Indeed, genuine political equality has been rejected by Americans as a proper principle of authority within firms. Hence the ownership and control of enterprises creates enormous inequalities among citizens in their capacities and opportunities for participating in *governing economic enterprises*.

It might be objected that massive departures from political equality in the government of the state and the internal government of firms are by no means an excessive price to pay for the achievements of corporate capitalism, an economic order that has managed better than any alternative to help sustain certain crucial values: not only greater efficiency in economic affairs than any of the alternatives but also in democratic countries a historically unusual, perhaps unique degree of democracy and political liberty in governing the state. Arguably, too, capitalism has helped to provide a much greater degree of liberty in economic life than any alternative has so far been able to produce.

In later chapters I want to consider whether it might not be possible to find an alternative to corporate

capitalism that would be just as efficient and would at
the same time enhance the values of democracy, political equality, and political liberty. Would any such
alternative, however, impair fundamental *economic liberties* more than corporate capitalism? The answer depends, of course, on what we mean by economic liberty, democracy, and the democratic process, and the
relative value we assign to each. It is a familiar con-
tention in the United States that a claim to economic
liberty is just as valid as a claim to political liberty or
to political equality, that economic liberty includes a
right to private property, that a right to private property includes the rights of private owners to control
or to delegate control over their firms more or less as
they see fit, and consequently that the corporate structure of modern American capitalism rests ultimately
on an "inalienable" right. Though views like this may
be less common than they once were in the United
States, and some Americans would reject them, they
continue to derive strength from traditional American beliefs about inalienable rights to life, liberty,
and—the last of the constitutional trio—property.

The Democratic Process

What then does a rational belief in democracy entail? The core of such a belief, it seems to me, is the
view that in a certain kind of human association, the
process of government should as far as possible meet
democratic criteria, because people involved in this

kind of association possess a *right*, an inalienable right to govern themselves by the democratic process.

Assumptions. The validity of a claim to this right rests on certain assumptions about the nature of a democratic association and the people in it. These are:

1. The collection of people in the association has a need to reach at least some collective decisions that will be binding on all the members of the collectivity.
2. These binding collective decisions involve at least two distinguishable stages: a period in which the agenda is set, followed at some point by a decisive stage of "final" decisions, after which the decision becomes binding on the members of the association.
3. Binding collective decisions ought to be made only by persons who are subject to the decisions— that is, by members of the association, not by persons outside the association. For laws cannot rightfully be imposed on others by persons who are not themselves obliged to obey those laws.
4. A weak principle of equality: The good of each person is entitled to equal consideration.
5. A principle of liberty: In general, each adult person in the association is entitled to be the final judge of his or her own interests. The burden of proof never lies with any adult person to demonstrate entitlement to this liberty. Instead the burden of proof must always lie with anyone who wishes to establish exceptions to the principle.
6. A strong principle of equality: With respect to all

matters, all the adult members of the association (the citizens of a government) are roughly equally well qualified to decide which matters do or do not require binding collective decisions. Those who participate shall decide which matters the demos (the citizenry) is best qualified to decide for itself; which matters, in the membership's view, the demos is not qualified to decide for itself; and the terms on which the demos will delegate a contingent and recoverable authority to others.

7. An elementary principle of fairness: In general, scarce and valued things should be fairly allocated. Fairness sometimes requires that each person's needs or deserts be taken into account. If needs or deserts are unequal, then a concern for equality in this sense— "person-regarding" equality—will often lead to a person receiving an unequal share or lot. In some circumstances, however, fairness requires that each person receive an equal share or an equal chance: here fairness means that equality must be "lot-regarding," not "person-regarding" (Rae 1981, 82–103). When the claims of different persons to a scarce and valued thing are equally valid, and no person's claim is better or worse than any other's, then if the thing is appropriately divisible into equal shares (as, for example, votes can be divided), each equally valid claimant is entitled to an equal *share*. If the thing to be allocated is not appropriately divisible into equal shares for allotment to each equally valid claim (as with a precious painting, for example, or an opportunity to speak at a very large meeting), then each equally valid

claimant is entitled to an equal *chance* to obtain whatever is allocated.

Criteria for a democratic process. Although I shall not do so here, it can be shown, I think, that any process for making binding collective decisions would be inconsistent with one or more of the preceding assumptions if, and to the extent that, it violated the following criteria (Dahl 1979):

1. Equal votes: The rule for determining outcomes at the decisive stage must take into account, and take equally into account, the expressed preferences of each citizen as to the outcome; that is, votes must be allocated equally among citizens.
2. Effective participation: Throughout the process of making binding collective decisions, each citizen must have an adequate and equal opportunity for expressing a preference as to the final outcome.
3. Enlightened understanding: In order to express preferences accurately, each citizen must have adequate and equal opportunities, within the time permitted by the need for a decision, for discovering and validating his or her preferences on the matter to be decided.
4. Final control of the agenda by the demos: The demos must have the exclusive opportunity to make decisions that determine what matters are and are not to be decided by processes that satisfy the first three criteria.
5. Inclusiveness: The demos must include all adult

members except transients and persons proven to be mentally defective.

These five criteria, I believe, fully specify the democratic process, for I am unable to see in what respects a process meeting these criteria would not be democratic, or how any process that failed to satisfy one or more of the criteria could be regarded as fully democratic. In the same way, I think the criteria fully specify what we mean by political equality, for political equals would surely be persons among whom the criteria are met—and to the extent the criteria are not met, then the persons could hardly be said to be politically equal.

Now a familiar objection to an assertion of this kind will be that what I have specified are criteria for merely "formal," not "real," political equality and the democratic process. Suppose citizens are highly unequal in their political resources—income, wealth, or status, for example. Would they not be unequal politically? Of course they might and very likely would be. But such an objection is nonetheless mistaken. For when differences in political resources cause citizens to be politically unequal, then that inequality necessarily reveals itself by a violation of the criteria.

I am going to suggest later on that both corporate capitalism and bureaucratic socialism tend to produce inequalities in social and economic resources so great as to bring about severe violations of political equality and hence of the democratic process, and that we ought to consider whether an alternative more congenial to democratic values might not be found. The alternative I want to explore is an extension of the democratic process to economic enterprises. A possible objection to such a proposal, which we may usefully anticipate here, is that while democracy may be justified in the government of the *state* because the preceding assumptions may apply to a state, democracy cannot be justified in the government of economic enterprises because not all the assumptions do apply.

The assumptions and the criteria I have just set forth do not, however, specify any particular kind of association. Instead, the democratic process, and only the democratic process, would be justified in *any* association for which the assumptions are valid. The justification for the democratic process is therefore contingent on judgments—practical, prudential, moral, or concrete—about a specific association, or a kind of association, and the qualities of the people who constitute it. I believe this degree of contingency in the argument cannot reasonably be avoided. The argument thus would not support a claim to democracy as absolute and universal, valid for all people, in all times and circumstances, or in all associations of every kind. What my argument does, however, is to establish a claim to democracy *as a matter of right* in *any* association of any kind for which the assumptions are valid. It would seem appropriate to say that in any association for which the assumptions are valid, the adult members possess an inalienable right to govern themselves by means of the democratic process, whether or not they choose to exercise that right.

The question, then, is whether the assumptions apply to the kind of an association formed by an economic enterprise, thus implying an entitlement to the democratic process in the government of the enterprise. Evidently, we need to examine whether we have sufficient grounds for believing, for example, that the decisions of business firms are "binding" on their employees in any way comparable to the laws of a state, a claim that on the face of it may seem absurd to many people, or, what will no doubt seem even more dubious, whether the strong principle of equality makes sense when applied to an economic enterprise.

We will return to these questions. But now that the meanings of political equality and the democratic process have been clarified, we need first to consider the relation between the democratic process and property rights, particularly when these are asserted with respect to a modern large corporation.

Property Rights Versus
the Democratic Process

A right to private ownership of an economic enterprise is usually defended on two grounds. An *instrumental*, or *utilitarian*, defense holds that, on balance, private ownership is beneficial—to people individually, to the society collectively, and to values such as efficiency, economic progress, political liberty, and so on. According to another familiar view, however, people are entitled to private ownership of property (and so to private ownership of economic enterprises) as a natural, even inalienable, *moral right*, which, like other natural rights, it is the duty of governments and laws to protect. The one argument does not exclude the other, and in the United States both have been used throughout the nation's history.

In prescribing that no person shall "be deprived of life, liberty, or property, without due process of law," the protections of the Fifth Amendment, and later the Fourteenth, could be justified on either ground, or both. Inevitably, cases arose under the new constitution that invited the justices of the Supreme Court to consider whether the constitutional compact was intended to protect a natural right to property and if so how far this natural right limited the regulatory authority of a legislature. For nearly a century the Court was moderately cautious about circumscribing the authority of state legislatures, or the Congress, to regulate economic enterprises. But from the mid 1870s onward, as the new corporate capitalism solidified its victory over the waning forces of agrarianism, the justices increasingly extended the scope of the new constitutional doctrine of "substantive due process" to protect business from regulation. (See, for example, Brest 1975, 705–54.)

However, although the two kinds of defense are often commingled, they carry radically different implications for the democratic process. If private ownership of economic enterprises is a purely instrumental arrangement, and self-government is a fundamental and inalienable right, then any legal entitlement to private ownership of the economy is *subordinate* to the right of self-government, and in a democratic coun-

try the people and their representatives would be
entitled to decide through the democratic process
how far any particular arrangement may, on balance,
achieve their values. They could decide that the private ownership of economic enterprises was desirable, that public or social ownership was preferable,
or that any one of an indefinite number of possible
combinations would be best.

But if, on the contrary, private ownership is a natural and inalienable right, then conceivably that right
might be *superior* to the right to self-government, and
a people might not be entitled to infringe that right
even through the democratic process. Although,
judged from a purely utilitarian perspective, the consequences of private property might sometimes be
harmful, it would not necessarily follow that a people
could properly claim the authority to regulate property so as to avoid these consequences. For example,
the fact that the ownership of property was highly
unequal would not by itself justify an attempt somehow to reallocate property so as to reduce inequality.
As the Supreme Court said in 1915 when it held unconstitutional a Kansas statute that prohibited contracts forbidding employees to join labor unions,

No doubt, wherever the right of private property exists,
there must and will be inequalities of fortune; and thus it
naturally happens that parties negotiating a contract are not
equally unhampered by circumstances. . . . And, since it is
self-evident that, unless things are held in common, some
persons must have more property than others, it is from
the nature of things impossible to uphold the freedom of
contract and the right of private property without at the

same time recognizing as legitimate those inequalities of fortune that are the necessary result of the exercise of those rights.

(*Coppage* v. *Kansas, 236 U.S. 1 [1915]; in Brest, 734*)

Do people possess a fundamental moral right to private property similar to their fundamental and inalienable right to self-government? If so, might not the two kinds of rights conflict with one another? And if so, is one superior to the other? Just as we examined the grounds that would justify a claim to a fundamental right to political equality and the democratic process, so now we need to explore the reasoning that would justify a fundamental right to property comparable—perhaps even superior—to the right to the democratic process.

From the beginning of our nation's existence, and indeed earlier, the question of the relative priority of democracy and property has received two fundamentally conflicting answers. The intensity of the conflict between these two discordant answers has been muted, however, by a background of agreement, an agreement that arose early and entered deeply into the American consciousness. In controversies over the relative priority of property and democracy in the first half century of the republic, spokesmen on both sides tended to assume that individuals have a natural right to property, and that, like other natural rights, the right to property ought to be protected by governments. Both sides were also inclined to believe that as a general matter power and property run together. Probably spokesmen for both sides would have agreed with Benjamin Leigh, a leader of the conservative pro-property forces in the Virginia Constitutional Convention of 1829–30:

"Power and property may be separated for a time, by force or fraud—but divorced, never. For, so soon as the pang of separation is felt . . . property will purchase power, or power will take property. And either way, there must be an end of free Government."

(in Peterson 1966, 338)

Nevertheless, the two sides disagreed over fundamental priorities. On the one side, supporters of property held that political equality must finally yield to property rights. In the famous trio of life, liberty, and property, property ought to take precedence.

"It does not follow," Leigh went on to assert, "that, because all men are born equal, and have equal rights to life, liberty, and the property they can acquire by honest industry, therefore, all men may rightly claim, in an established society, equal political powers—especially, equal power to dispose of the property of others.

(Peterson, 347–48)

Those who supported the goal of democracy insisted, on the contrary, that a person's right to self-government, and thus to political equality, was more fundamental than the right to property. Although Jefferson may have vacillated, his settled view seems to have been that the right to property is more social than natural, that property is not so much prior to society as dependent on it.

"It is a moot question," he wrote several years before his death, "whether the origin of any kind of property is derived from nature at all. . . . Stable ownership is the gift of social law, and is given late in the progress of society."

(Schlatter 1951, 198)

This subordination of property to society is consistent with Jefferson's conspicuous omission of property a half century earlier in his claim that among the inherent and inalienable rights with which all men are endowed by their creator are life, liberty, and the pursuit of happiness (Wills, 1978, 237–38).

From time to time political controversy was bound to evoke these contrasting views. Perhaps the conflict was never clearer than in several of the state constitutional conventions of the 1820s, at which property requirements for the suffrage were challenged.

"The tendency of universal suffrage," Chancellor Kent flatly declared at the New York Convention of 1821, "is to jeopardize the rights of property, and the principles of liberty. The notion that every man that works a day on the road, or serves an idle hour in the militia, is entitled as of right to an equal participation in the whole power of government, is most unreasonable, and has no foundation of justice."

(Peterson, 194–95)

Conservatives like Kent in New York, Story in Massachusetts, and Leigh in Virginia who sought to protect the privileges of property against the claims of democracy were, as we all know, defeated, and rather easily. Their defeat was a skirmish in the larger

advance toward decisive victory of a democratic ideology that offered an enduring solution to the conflict
between property and democracy. That solution involved nothing less than the elimination altogether of
the conflict.

From ancient times, political theorists have commonly supposed that a conflict between democracy
and property rights would tend to arise only if property were unequally distributed; the greater the inequality, presumably the greater the chance of conflict. One might call this the classical republican
problem of distributing power and property. Yet this
problem can be understood in two ways: Democracy
may be seen as a danger to property rights; or property rights may be seen as a danger to democracy. In
the first view, the task is to secure property rights,
and the danger comes from political equality. For if
citizens are politically equal but economically unequal, the less advantaged will combine against the
more advantaged; and if the less advantaged are the
more numerous, then the democratic process will enable them to injure the property rights of the more
advantaged. A majority made up of the less prosperous will be able to use their equality in the state to
appropriate the property of the wealthier minority.

The second view, in contrast, posits the danger ap-
proaching from the opposite direction. Economic resources are to some extent convertible into political resources. If citizens are unequal in economic
resources, so are they likely to be unequal in political
resources; and political equality will be impossible to
achieve. In the extreme case, a minority of rich will
possess so much greater political resources than other
citizens that they will control the state, dominate the

majority of citizens, and empty the democratic process of all content.

The only solution consistent with republican government was then obvious: somehow economic resources had to be distributed more or less evenly—evenly enough at any rate to avoid significant numbers of poor and rich. We might call this the classical republican solution, one which political theorists sympathetic to popular government, from Aristotle to Rousseau, adopted.

These classical views on property distribution were accepted by both sides in the early American debates over property versus democracy. Each side, however, saw danger coming from the opposite direction. In the Massachusetts Convention of 1820–21, after lauding the blessings of property, Justice Story (then at the beginning of his long career) called attention to the classical republican problem:

"Universal suffrage . . . could not long exist in a community where there was great inequality of property. The holders of estates would be obliged in such case, either in some way to restrain the right of suffrage, or else such right of suffrage would ere long divide the property. In the nature of things, those who have not property, and see their neighbors possess much more than they think them to need, cannot be favorable to laws made for the protection of property.

(in Peterson, 100)

Both sides tended to agree, however, that the best solution would be a wide diffusion of economic resources, which in the United States meant property. Indeed, Story held it to be "the part of political wis-

dom to found government on property; and to establish such distribution of property, by the laws which
regulate its transmission and alienation, as to interest
the great majority of society in the protection of the
government. This is, I imagine, the true theory and
the actual practice in our republican institutions" (Peterson, 100). This view is not unlike Jefferson's point
that while "an equal division of property is imprac-
ticable . . . legislators cannot invent too many de-
vices for subdividing property" (Schlatter, 196). Thus
both sides adopted the classical republican solution.

Both sides agreed, then, that in order to ensure
the wide diffusion of property an American republic
would require, some regulation would be needed. It
is easy to see, however, that the extent of the regulation a democratic country might require depends on
the initial distribution of property in that country and
the extent to which the economic order itself, independent of any regulation, generates equality or inequality in the distribution of property. If conditions
naturally produce and can be expected to continue
producing a wide diffusion of economic resources
that is sufficient to promote and sustain political equality, then little or no regulation by the polity would be
necessary. The task of ensuring a favorable and relatively diffuse distribution of property would, in effect, take care of itself—the ideal circumstance for the
classical republican solution.

We might call a system of this kind a *self-regulating
egalitarian order*. Without excessive exaggeration, this
lucky circumstance can be likened to the conditions
among Americans—or rather white male Americans—that Tocqueville describes in *Democracy in Amer-*

ica. About the time he visited the United States, American conditions had already so nearly approached the classical republican solution that the fears of conservatives like Story, Kent, and Leigh sounded like old men's nightmares. The ideology of agrarian democratic republicanism was triumphant, and that ideology held out the promise of a republic of farmers among whom landed property would be widely dispersed. This possibility was in substantial part a result not of a deliberate collective decision but of what Tocqueville called "accidental" causes. Americans had access to a vast supply of land which with a modicum of guile, fraud, violence, and blunder could be removed from the control of its original inhabitants, particularly since their "control" was often exercised with a light hand by a very small population. Although dispersion of ownership might require some regulation, it would not need much. Even the Homestead Act was late and somewhat ineffectual. It arrived not at the dawn of the American agrarian republic but a little past noon, when the agrarian sun had already passed its zenith; and it made but a modest contribution to farm ownership—supplying only 600,000 out of an increase of nearly 4 million farms between 1860 and 1900, and only 80 million out of more than 430 million acres added to total land in farms during that period (Blum et al. 1963, 407).

But the conditions of Americans in Tocqueville's time were historically exceptional, and few other countries have been so lucky. American luck ran out when an economic order that had generated a fair degree of equality among white male citizens without much planning, regulation, or deliberate collective

decision was replaced by the revolutionary new order
of corporate capitalism. By 1900 and even before, it
was increasingly evident that the ideology of agrarian
democratic republicanism had developed during a pe-
culiar moment in world history—a moment of extraordinary importance, but a moment nonetheless.
For the agrarian socioeconomic order was destined to
be wholly superseded by corporate capitalism. And
as an unregulated external force, corporate capitalism
would automatically generate acute inequalities in the
distribution of property as well as other social and
economic resources.

Yet in what John M. Blum has rightly called "one
of the strangest reversals in the history of political
thought," the new partisans of property—who in
their loyalty to property over democracy were the
successors of Story, Kent, and Leigh—transformed
many of the key ideas of the dominant democratic
ideology into a justification of the new economic order. "Man became economic man, democracy was
identified with capitalism, liberty with property and
the use of it, equality with opportunity for gain, and
progress with economic change and the accumulation
of capital" (Blum et al., 432).

What is most significant for our purposes, these
new radical conservatives were amazingly successful
in transferring to corporate property the ideological
justification for private ownership that was at the
heart of the older ideology of agrarian democratic re-
publicans. Much as a new political regime may sometimes inherit the legitimacy of the old regime it su-
persedes, so the legitimacy of private property, which
was deeply embedded in the older ideology and in

American consciousness, was transferred to the new economic order. The transfer was so complete that corporate property came to enjoy fewer fundamental challenges in the United States than perhaps in any other country in the world, and certainly than in any European country. From *Lochner* v. *New York* in 1905 (198 U.S. 45) to *Morehead* v. *Tipaldo* in 1936 (298 U.S. 587), the United States Supreme Court actively assisted in the process of ideological transfer by granting to corporations constitutional immunities from state and federal regulations.

Thus an economic order that spontaneously produced inequality in the distribution of economic and political resources acquired legitimacy, at least in part, by clothing itself in the recut garments of an outmoded ideology in which private ownership was justified on the ground that a wide diffusion of property would support political equality. As a consequence, Americans have never asked themselves steadily or in large numbers whether an alternative to corporate capitalism might be more consistent with their commitment to democracy.

Corporate Capitalism and the Right to Private Property

Consider the following argument:

1. Everyone has a right to economic liberty.
2. The right to economic liberty justifies a right to private property.

3. A right to private property justifies a right to private ownership of economic enterprises.

4. A right to privately owned economic enterprises justifies privately owned corporations of great size.

5. A right to private ownership of corporate enterprises cannot properly be curtailed by the democratic process.

The last four statements involve non sequiturs. For example, the final proposition involves a non sequitur because the term *right* is ambiguous. A right may be legal but not constitutionally guaranteed, like the right smokers once had to smoke in restaurants and other public places. A right may be constitutionally protected but not moral, like the right to own slaves in Virginia before the Civil War. If a legal system violates a fundamental moral right, then to that extent we ought to condemn the legal order as an improper violation of a fundamental moral right and seek to change it. The right to self-government, and thus to the democratic process, is surely one of the most fundamental of all moral rights. Whether private ownership of economic enterprises is also a fundamental moral right is precisely the issue. If it is not, then the fifth statement above is a non sequitur.

But I do not see how private ownership of corporate enterprise can be a fundamental moral right. To reach such a conclusion requires jumping a series of logical hurdles. Even if we were to assume that everyone has a fundamental moral right to economic liberty, it would not follow that everyone has a fundamental moral right to private property. Even if we were to assume that everyone has a fundamental moral right to private property, it would not follow that economic enterprises should be privately owned. Even if we were to assume that economic enterprises should be privately owned, it would not follow that they should be owned privately and managed in the interests of shareholders—much less managed in the interests of managers. We cannot leap from my entitlement to secure possession of the shirt on my back or the cash in my pocket to a fundamental moral right to acquire shares in IBM and therewith the standard rights of ownership that shareholdings legally convey.

But, one may object, isn't property a natural right, as Locke contended? Don't we have a moral right to life, liberty, and property?

To assert that private property is a natural right is, standing alone, to say close to nothing at all. To begin with, the truth of the assertion is certainly not self-evident. Moreover, even if it were true, a natural right to property might conflict with other natural rights. From the bald assertion of property as a natural right we cannot know whether it is subordinate to a natural right to self-government, as Jefferson thought, or superior, as Kent and Story claimed. Nor would such a natural right, standing alone, sustain a claim to private ownership of economic enterprises.

A final difficulty besets all claims to property as a fundamental right equal or superior to the right to self-government. As every law student learns, the legal right to property is not a single right; it is a bundle of rights, privileges, duties, and liabilities. What has been called the "full" or "liberal" concept of ownership entails the right to possess, or "exclusive physical control of the thing owned"; the right to use; the right to manage; the right to the income from the thing owned; the right to the capital, that is, "the power to alienate the thing and to consume, waste, modify, or destroy it"; the right to security from expropriation; the power of transmissibility; the absence of term to one's ownership rights; "the duty to forbear from using the thing in certain ways harmful to others"; "liability to having the thing taken away for repayment of debt"; and "the existence of rules governing the reversion of lapsed ownership rights" (Honoré, cited in Becker 1977, 19). If the assertion of a natural right to property is meant to include all these features, then the claim is so broad that a great deal of what is legally and conventionally regarded as private property would not satisfy it; and we should have to conclude that no legal system has ever fully sustained the claim of a natural right to property. Conversely, if the prohibition of harmful use is broadly interpreted, then the scope of the natural right to property may be so narrow and the scope for regulation so extensive as to make the claim nearly meaningless. In the end, then, a mere claim to private property as a natural right gets us nowhere. We are entitled not only to a reasoned justification, and not a mere assertion, but also to some specification of the scope of such a right.

I am not aware of any reasoned justification for

private property and a specification of its scope that would also justify a claim to private ownership of enterprises in existing corporate form. Robert Nozick's entitlement theory, for example, is too narrow to justify corporate property. His theory asserts that no one is entitled to a holding (property) except by repeated applications of two principles: the holding must originally have been justly acquired, and it must have been justly transferred from someone originally entitled to the holding. As an escape route for holdings wrongfully acquired or transferred, Nozick permits, and indeed requires, rectification of past injustices (1974, 150–53). But no one with the barest knowledge of the history of economic enterprises in this country, and probably any other, would want to contend, I think, that corporate holdings meet Nozick's rigorous requirements. Nor does Nozick himself advance such a claim. If American corporate enterprises were required either to pass Nozick's tests or to divest themselves of their property, we would witness a vast divestiture, and either descendents of the first occupiers would acquire ownership of much of our real property or they would have to be richly compensated. Certainly American corporate capitalism bears scant resemblance to Nozick's own framework for Utopia.

Labor theories of property acquisition are at once too narrow and too broad. Locke's theory, for example, is too narrow because it requires a person to take no more than he can use and to leave "enough, and as good" for others (Locke [1689] 1970, 306), but it is simultaneously too broad.

Though the Earth, and all inferior Creatures be common
to all Men, yet every Man has *Property* in his own *Person*.
This no Body has any Right to but himself. The *Labor* of
his Body, and the *Work* of his Hands, we may say, are properly his. Whatsoever then he removes out of the State that
Nature hath provided, and left it in, he hath mixed his *Labor* with, and joined to it something that is his own, and
thereby makes it his Property.

(Locke, 305–6)

Whatever one may think of the validity of Locke's
notion of labor as justifying private property, and
there are good reasons for rejecting it (cf. Becker,
32–48), it cannot justify the ownership of a corporation by stockholders. For on Locke's justification,
only those who labor to produce goods and services,
the workers and employees, would be entitled to own
the goods and services produced by a firm. Moreover, no one would be entitled to own land or to gain
rent from land; at most, those who labored to improve it would be entitled to the fruit of their labor.

Nor does corporate property fare better on Mill's
justification, for his requirements are too stringent. In
his view you are entitled to own a thing that would
not otherwise have existed except for your labor, provided also that your labor is "beyond what is required,
morally, that one do for others" and "others lose
nothing by being excluded from [it]," (Becker, 41).
Mill's justification not only excludes property in land
but, like Locke, limits initial acquisition to producers.
Thus his defense, like Locke's, is both too narrow and
too broad to justify private ownership of corporations
by stockholders.

Ownership (and nominal control) of firms by stock-holders is often held to be justified on both practical and moral grounds. The practical ground is the need for capital. The practical question, however, is whether those who provide capital must necessarily own and control the enterprises to which they supply capital. In principle, the task of supplying capital to enterprises can be separated from the rights of owner-ship and control. In practice, capital supplied through loans and bonds does not entail ownership and con-trol of the enterprises that take on the debt. Even in some countries with corporate capitalist economies, such as Japan and West Germany, financial institu-tions provide a much larger share of capital, and equity a correspondingly smaller share, than in the United States. Obviously any alternative to corporate capitalism would have to solve the practical prob-lem of how capital is to be supplied to economic enterprises.

But the question at issue here is not whether eco-nomic enterprises need capital, for of course they do, or whether practical alternatives to stockholder own-ership and control can be found, but whether any al-ternative to ownership and nominal control by stock-holders would necessarily violate some fundamental moral claim.

Ownership by stockholders is sometimes said to be justified on the grounds that stockholders are morally entitled to a reward for sacrificing the use of their money. But what do they sacrifice? To reply that they sacrifice other opportunities for investment is to beg the question; for the question is precisely whether they are entitled to a reward from their investment.

To say that they sacrifice consumption is laughable, given the concentration of corporate ownership in the hands of institutions and wealthy investors. Even more telling, the argument from sacrifice would at most justify a return for the sacrifice; it would not justify control. I would suppose that workers sacrifice more of their lives by working than investors sacrifice by investing. Finally, the argument risks circularity unless it is so narrowly applied that it will no longer serve to justify the present structure of ownership in the United States. If I am robbed, and if the thief then agrees with me to take only half my money and leave me the other half, our agreement would have neither moral nor legal force, as the thief would discover if he were caught. So, too, if owners invest returns from previously owned property, then unless they were entitled to that previously owned property they are not entitled to a return from their present investment. Thus to say that they are entitled to a return because they sacrifice the use of their money begs the precise question at issue: whether, if their money represents a return from property ownership, they are entitled to that money.

Private property is sometimes defended as necessary to liberty. If what is meant is that everyone has a natural liberty to acquire and possess private property, and that it is therefore unjustifiable to impair this natural liberty, then the conclusion is assumed in the premise, and we remain with the bald unsupported assertion of a natural right. If what is meant is that everyone has a fundamental moral right to do what he or she chooses, so long as one does not infringe on the rights of others, then the argument begs the question at hand. Lawrence Becker, who attempts to derive property rights from political liberty, admits that the minimal

features of any system of political liberty adequate to provide a general justification for property produce significant restrictions on what can legitimately be owned—and in what ways it can be owned. Wherever a resource necessary for survival is scarce or nonrenewable, or exhaustible by appropriation or misuse, unrestricted ownership will not be compatible with the general justification of property (from liberty). Further, where a thing can be used to interfere with another's liberty to survive, ownership rights will have to be restricted. . . . More extensive systems of liberty . . . will place even further restrictions on ownership.
(Becker, 77–78)

If only because most resources "necessary for survival" are scarce, the argument would hardly be sufficient to justify private ownership of economic enterprises and might be used to dispute it.

A much stronger justification of property derived from political liberty is the argument that the exercise of political liberties typically requires the use of resources, and consequently a sure and protected access to resources is a necessary condition for the exercise of political liberty. I believe this argument is valid. But at most it would justify what I earlier called economic liberty, not private property, and certainly not private ownership of economic enterprises. Moreover, like many of the other arguments, it would justify access to a minimum supply of resources—the minimum required for the exercise of democratic rights, for example—but not the right to acquire an indefinitely large supply of resources.

A final justification for private property is furnished by utilitarian arguments. But the difficulty with utilitarian arguments is that they require a host of assumptions as to facts. An argument from utility can never establish a right as natural, inalienable, or indefeasible. For a right that may be justified as useful given one set of facts will have to be condemned as harmful given another set. On a utilitarian view, then, corporate capitalism, private ownership of economic enterprises, and even the institution of private property cannot be defended by appealing to fundamental rights. The only issue is their utility, compared with other possible solutions, after taking into account their consequences for the full range of relevant values: their effects on the democratic process, political equality, political rights, justice, efficiency, and economic freedom.

The conclusions to be drawn from this discussion of property are, it seems to me, these:

None of the well-known reasoned arguments for private property as a fundamental right, comparable to the fundamental right to self-government, is satisfactory, either because the grounds are unsatisfactory, or the scope of the right is unsatisfactorily defined, or both.

Nor do any of the reasoned arguments for private property justify a right to the unlimited acquisition of private property. If anything, they would justify a right to a minimum collection of resources, particularly the resources necessary to life, liberty, the pursuit of happiness, the democratic process, and primary rights.

And none of the reasoned arguments for private property as a right successfully justifies private ownership of corporate enterprises.

Consequently, the demos and its representatives are entitled to decide by means of the democratic process how economic enterprises should be owned and controlled in order to achieve, so far as may be possible, such values as democracy, fairness, efficiency, the cultivation of desirable human qualities, and an entitlement to such minimal personal resources as may be necessary to a good life.

3

Democracy and the Economic Order

What kind of economic order would best achieve the values of democracy, political equality, and liberty discussed in the previous chapters? To answer this question, I invite you to imagine that we are not only strongly committed to these values but also at an unusual historical juncture at which we confront an exceptional opportunity to create a new economic order for ourselves. What sort of economic order, we now ask ourselves, should we try to create?

Five Goals

Because we wish to achieve political equality, the democratic process, and primary political rights, we insist that our economic order must help to bring about these values, or at the very least not impair them. Among other things, then, the best economic order would help to generate a distribution of political resources favorable to the goals of voting equality, effective participation, enlightened understanding, and final control of the political agenda by all adults subject to the laws. Possibly several different distributions would be about equally satisfactory. Moreover, we are aware that critical political resources include not only economic resources like income and wealth but also knowledge and skills, and the special authority possessed by officials to employ the resources and capacities available to the government of the state.

If we had no other ends than the democratic process, then the requirements of that process would, quite properly, completely dominate our thinking about the economic order. But we may reasonably demand that our economic order also be *just*. To be sure, political equality is a form of distributive justice: if my argument in Chapter 2 is correct, then democracy, political equality, and the protection of primary political rights are necessary for a just distribution of authority. But the claims of justice reach beyond authority to the distribution of other rights, duties, benefits, disadvantages, opportunities, and claims. Among the spheres to which the requirements of justice apply is, of course, the distribution of economic resources—that is, economic fairness. Now it is conceivable that the distribution of economic resources required for democracy might also prove to be identical with the distribution required to achieve economic fairness. If so, solving the one problem would simultaneously solve the other. But this happy coincidence is by no means certain, and probably rather unlikely. Consequently we would want to satisfy ourselves that our economic order is fair. For, believing

as we do in fairness, or justice, it would be an un-
happy contradiction if our political order were fair
but our economic order grossly unfair.

Attractive as the goals of democracy and economic
fairness are to us, we would be irrational if we were
to neglect a third goal. We should also insist that our
economic order be *efficient*, that it would tend to minimize the ratio of valued inputs to valued outputs. For
if it were inefficient, then we would needlessly squan-
der our scarce resources and so live more poorly than
we need—which is irrational. If we could choose between an economic order that sustains democracy
and justice and would also be efficient, or an economic order that could achieve a like degree of democracy and justice but would be highly inefficient,
to choose the second rather than the first a people
would have to be much more foolish than I am assuming us to be. We would want to distinguish, however, between two kinds of outputs: outputs we as
consumers value and outputs we as producers value—
or, if you like, values realized in consuming end products and values realized in creating, producing, and
distributing end products.

Now suppose that our present economic order and
the new one we propose to create prove to be pretty
much alike in physical inputs and outputs, productivity, and per capita gross national product, as these are
conventionally measured, but differ in some crucial
respects in economic institutions. Suppose that at present work is a disagreeable burden for most people;
then suppose that by a crucial change in economic institutions work were to become a source of deep and

daily satisfaction for most of us. Even if other outputs and inputs were not thereby affected, would we not become a much richer country than we were? Would not our new economic order be more efficient in creating value than the old?

A fourth goal might now occur to us, and almost certainly would occur to any among us who had read Aristotle, say, or John Stuart Mill. We might want to apply to economic institutions the criterion that Mill proposed for judging a good form of government:

The most important point of excellence which any form of government can possess is to promote the virtue and intelligence of the people themselves. The first question in respect to any political institutions is how far they tend to foster in the members of the community the various desirable qualities, moral and intellectual . . .

(Mill [1861] 1958, 25)

Although this goal is inescapably vague, and both virtue and intelligence are sharply contested concepts, we would hardly disagree on the proposition that if one of two alternative economic orders tended to strengthen beliefs and conduct upholding personal honesty, say, or a willingness to assume responsibility for the foreseeable consequences of one's actions, while the other encouraged deceitfulness and irresponsibility, and if the two economic orders otherwise produced pretty much the same results, then the first would be definitely better than the second.

Even with these four goals, we would hardly exhaust the universe of values relevant to our economy.

Each of us has many other fundamental interests, goals, desires, wants, and values. An economic order that allowed us to achieve our various other goals, and in this sense to expand our freedom, would be better than one that prevented us from doing so. In our economic order, therefore, we will want each of us to be free to acquire whatever economic resources are necessary, and so far as possible sufficient, to advance and protect all our fundamental interests—or if you like, the economic resources necessary for a good life. Suppose we call these our *personal* economic resources. Perhaps we cannot say exactly how great or of what specific kinds our personal economic resources ought to be, but it would seem clear that we must have a right to gain access to adequate personal economic resources. This right may be what we mean when we use expressions like *economic freedom* and *economic liberty*. At a minimum, a right to economic freedom would guarantee a negative freedom: that is, no one would have the right to prevent any other person from exercising the right to acquire personal economic resources whenever an opportunity exists to exercise that right in a way that is not harmful to the equal right of another. At a maximum, such a right would guarantee positive economic freedom; that is, our social and economic order would ensure that such opportunities actually existed for each of us.

A right to economic freedom might lead to results that would fit perfectly with our other goals, but it is not obvious that this must be the case. We recognize, then, that our various goals might not be perfectly consistent and consequently we may often have to make judgments about trade-offs. Often our binding collective decisions as to public policies would require such judgments about trade-offs, and we would want to be able to make those judgments through the democratic process. We would therefore want to ensure that in accepting trade-offs among our goals we did not seriously impair the democratic process.

If these were our paramount values, what sort of an economic order would we try to construct? To answer this question I am going to make some assumptions that I shall not attempt to justify here. They are, however, highly plausible and may need no further justification.

To begin with, I assume that after contemplating the large body of historical experience with bureaucratic socialism in this century, we would judge it to be fundamentally inconsistent with our goals. In fact, I assume that we would reject any alternative that required highly concentrated power in the hands of central officials of the state. I assume, then, that to people with the five goals I have just described, a desirable economic order would disperse power, not concentrate it. Although important aspects of economic life would be subject to central controls (which I address in Chapter 5), in order to disperse power, control over many important decisions would have to be decentralized among a comparatively large number of relatively, though not completely, autonomous enterprises. In order for decentralization of control to be significant, decisions about inputs, outputs, prices, wages, and the allocation of any surplus would have to be made mainly or entirely at the level of the individual enterprises.

To achieve a satisfactory level of efficiency, however, the decisions of these relatively autonomous enterprises would somehow have to be coordinated. In an economy as complex as ours, I assume that coordination would require a market system, which would function as a critical external limit on enterprise decisions. For many reasons, such as avoiding undesirable externalities like pollution and preventing collusion among enterprises to exploit consumers, we would also want to establish a democratically controlled regulatory framework of laws and rules, within which the enterprises would operate.

In brief, we would search for an economic order that would decentralize many significant decisions among relatively autonomous economic enterprises, which would operate within limits set by a system of markets, and such democratically imposed laws, rules, and regulations as we may believe are necessary to achieve our goals. Such decentralization would require that significant authority to make important decisions be exercised *within* firms. The question we must therefore confront is, How should this authority be exercised within firms? I assume that we would reject the notion that firms should be simply extensions of the central bureaucracy of the state—that all significant authority within firms should be exercised hierarchically by state officials. I also assume that we would search for an alternative to corporate capitalism, where authority within firms is exercised hierarchically by managers nominally accountable to stock-holders. Our problem, then, is to discover a better alternative.

Sketch of an Alternative

I now want to consider a possible alternative: a system of economic enterprises collectively owned and democratically governed by all the people who work in them.[1] By democratically governed, I mean that within each enterprise decision making would be designed so far as possible to satisfy the criteria for the democratic process that I described in the preceding chapter, and thereby to achieve political equality and the protection of primary political rights within the firm. One crucially important feature of self-governing enterprises, then, is that they satisfy the criterion of voting equality; hence each person employed in an enterprise is entitled to one and only one vote. Systems of this kind have been called workers' cooperatives or examples of self-management or industrial democracy; but I prefer the term *self-governing enterprises*.[2] Since such an enterprise, like a local gov-

1. In clarifying my ideas on this question I have profited greatly from a number of unpublished papers by David Ellerman, cited in the bibliography, as well as numerous discussions with and papers by students in my graduate seminar on The Government of Economic Enterprises and my undergraduate seminar on Democracy at Work.

2. Although in ordinary American usage both *workers* and *employees* are equivalent to "all persons who work directly for wages or salaries in an organization," distinctions between the two are

ernment, is democratic within limits set by external democratic political controls and by markets, the people who work in the firm might be called citizens of the enterprise.

Because the firm is controlled democratically, the enterprise's citizens determine how the revenues of the firm are to be allocated. Obviously their abstract freedom to allocate the firm's revenues is limited by the need to buy inputs and sell outputs at prices they cannot, except sometimes perhaps in the very short run, unilaterally determine; and by the need to attract and hold a work force; for to use Albert Hirschman's creative distinction, workers may influence the decisions of the enterprise by exit as well as voice (Hirschman 1970). Within the enterprise, its citizens (or their elected representatives or managers to whom they delegate authority) determine wages and decide how surplus revenues are to be allocated. They therefore determine how much is to be set aside for reinvestment, how much is to be distributed to the enterprise's citizens, and the principle according to which these distributions are made.

Such a system of self-governing enterprises should not be confused with others that it might vaguely or closely resemble. Obviously self-governing enterprises only remotely resemble pseudodemocratic

---

sometimes intended. Here, however, I use the two words interchangeably. Advocates of self-managed enterprises sometimes distinguish between labor-managed and worker-managed systems, but the distinctions are not uniform (Vanek 1975; see also his earlier description: Vanek 1970, 6–7; Schweickart 1980, 52–53; Selucky 1979, 180).

schemes of employee consultation by management; schemes of limited employee participation that leave all the crucial decisions with a management elected by stockholders; or Employee Stock Ownership Plans (ESOPs) that are created only or primarily to provide corporations with low-interest loans, lower corporate income taxes, greater cash flow, employee pension plans, or a market for their stock (Comptroller General 1980, 37 and passim), without, however, any significant changes in control.[3]

While self-governing enterprises may prove to have several advantages over not only the typical stockholder-owned and management-controlled corporation but also publicly owned and hierarchically run firms, the justification most relevant here is the contribution they might make to the values of justice and democracy. If they were about as efficient as present firms, if they did not diminish fundamental liberties, and if at the same time they were superior in their consequences for democracy and justice, then they would be definitely better. What consequences for de-

3. According to one estimate, 3,000 firms had ESOPs by 1978. Only about ninety could be identified in which "a majority of the equity is owned by a majority of the employees." Moreover, firms owned by employees through ESOPs "concentrate ownership in managers, since most distribute stock according to salary to qualify for certain tax benefits" (Select Committee on Small Business 1979, 2). An ESOP could, however, serve as a means to a self-governing enterprise if the employees acquired a majority of voting stock that would be held in trust and voted as a block by employees on the basis of one person, one vote. In 1980 the Rath Packing Company was reorganized in this way (Gunn 1981, 17–21).

mocracy and justice could we reasonably expect from a system of self-governing enterprises?

We need to appraise two different kinds of arguments based on democratic values. First, that democracy within firms would improve the quality of democracy in the government of the state by transforming us into better citizens and by facilitating greater political equality among us. Second, that if democracy is justified in the government of our state, then it is also justified in the governments that make decisions *within* firms (quite apart from any benefits entailed by the preceding argument).

The first argument is more usual among democratic theorists than the second. I now turn to that argument, leaving consideration of the second argument for the next two chapters.

Democratic Citizens Through Participatory Democracy?

Self-government in economic enterprises is often advocated as a way of creating "participatory democracy" and producing changes in human personalities and behavior that, it is said, participation will bring about. In this perspective, the ideal of the polis is transferred to the workplace, and the enterprise becomes a site for fulfilling Rousseau's vision of political society (as expressed in the *Social Contract*) or for meeting Mill's criterion of excellence for a government—"that it should promote the virtue and intelligence of the people themselves." Workplace democracy, it is sometimes claimed, will foster human development, enhance the sense of political efficacy, reduce alienation, create a solidary community based on work, strengthen attachments to the general good of the community, weaken the pull of self-interest, produce a body of active and concerned public-spirited citizens within the enterprises, and stimulate greater participation and better citizenship in the government of the state itself (e.g., Wootton 1966; Pateman 1970; and Mason 1982). Should we expect a system of self-governing enterprises to transform human beings in these ways—to make them more democratic, politically active, social, public-spirited, cooperative, concerned for the general good?

The hope for human regeneration through changes in political, economic, and social structures exerts a magical power on the utopian imagination. Forecasts of a new human being produced by structural changes have been made not only by advocates of workplace democracy, but by many others: liberals like Mill, as well as communists, socialists, fascists, and Nazis. Yet these forecasts seem to be regularly discredited by experience—at least in those cases when journalists and scholars have been able to assess that experience. Thus we have not heard much in recent years about the New Soviet Man, while the Chinese worker or peasant who was to consider only the good of the whole society has been replaced in ideology and practice by workers and peasants motivated largely by material incentives. Meanwhile, however, some writers continue to promise that workplace democ-

racy would transform workers into much more vir-
tuous citizens.

The evidence, although incomplete, is mixed. In a
study of a Los Angeles high-fidelity equipment manufacturing firm with about a thousand employees,
John F. Witte found that the introduction of a planning council, a number of special committees, and
work teams, all of which greatly increased opportunities for participation in decisions, led over a fourteen-
month period to only a modest increase in average
participation. More to the point, increased participation by activists did not reduce their alienation from
work; in fact, while alienation decreased for participants in work teams, it increased for participants on
the planning council and the special committees. Neither the new opportunities for participation nor participation itself brought about an increase in support
for participation. Support actually declined among
the activists, partly because of "the disenchantment
felt by some council members at the apparent apathy
of their fellow workers" (Witte 1980, 149). In a
comparison of attitudes among workers in plywood
cooperatives in the Pacific Northwest and in conventional (unionized) plywood firms, Edward S. Greenberg found that

the expectation held by many theorists of industrial democracy that self-managed work environments might serve to
nurture feelings of cooperation, equality, generosity, and
self-confidence in one's fellows is only partly met within
the plywood cooperatives. The expectation that such feelings would spill over the walls of the workplace so as to

incorporate society, economy, and government is decidedly *not* met. . . . Indeed, the findings point to the opposite results.

(*Greenberg 1981, p. 40*)

In Yugoslavia, the system of self-management has not yet brought about very high levels of political participation, and, as in the United States, the tendency of political participation to increase with a person's level of socioeconomic resources remains relatively strong (Verba, Nie, and Kim 1978, 57–79, 292–93; Verba and Shabad 1978; but see also Oleszczuk 1978). The Yugoslav scholar Josip Obradovic observed a strong tendency for participation in workers' councils to be dominated by experts and managers (Obradovic 1972; Bertsch and Obradovic n.d.). Like Witte he also found that "participants in self-management are *more* alienated than nonparticipants. Possibly for these workers the direct experience with self-management has been so frustrating that their sense of alienation has become even greater" (Obradovic 1970, 165). One source of their frustrations may well be the tendency of managers to dominate the councils.

Against these findings, however, are some that support at least modest expectations for positive changes. In a study of a West Coast plant producing a "paper-based consumer product" with about 225 employees, J. Maxwell Elden concluded that workplace democracy increased satisfaction, personal growth, and satisfaction with opportunities for self-management; these changes in turn increased political efficacy and

social participation (Elden 1981). Several other studies have led to similar conclusions (these are summarized by Elden, 53–54; see also Bermeo 1982).

Such evidence as we now have does not, I think,
warrant high hopes for huge changes in attitudes, values, and character from greater democracy at work. It
should be said, however, that all the present evidence
is very short-term, since it is derived from studies
of workers who were already rather fully formed
by their society. We cannot confidently predict what
changes in character or personality might ensue, not
in the short space of months or years, but over many
generations. I cannot help thinking that if their experiment in self-management lasts a hundred years, Yu-
goslavs will be different in important ways from what
they would have been had they continued to live in a
command society that was authoritarian not only in
politics but in economic life as well. And might not
we Americans be different, if in the 1880s we had
adopted self-governing enterprises rather than corporate capitalism as the standard solution?

Moral responsibility.   Although the consequences for
democratic character are problematical, a system of
self-governing enterprises does promise one change
of some importance for the quality of a people. Com-
plexity and giantism have created such a distance between our actions and their consequences that our
capacity for moral action has been dangerously im-
poverished. Moral action requires an opportunity and
a capacity for understanding the consequences of one's
actions and for assuming responsibility for those con-

sequences. Yet when the organizations and other structures in which we make our choices encourage us to displace the adverse consequences on others, while we reap only the benefits, then to say that we are ultimately "responsible" for the consequences of our actions is little more than a philosophical abstraction. Just as guardianship in the government of the state robs a people of its opportunities and capacities for responsibility, so too does guardianship in the government of a firm. Moreover, the structure of American corporate enterprise narrows the domain of moral responsibility to the vanishing point.[4]

On our assumptions, self-governing enterprises would operate within a market. It would therefore be a mistake to suppose that they could—or even should—entirely escape pressures toward instrumental rationality and protection of the firm's revenues. It is too much to expect, then, that self-governing enterprises would always act to prevent the displacement of adverse consequences on others. Consequently, like cor-

4. As an example, in 1983 the U.S. federal government in a civil suit against General Motors (GM) contended that the company had sold 1980 X-model cars knowing the cars had hazardous brake defects. The government also contended that requests for information by the Department of Transportation's Office of Defects Investigation from 1980 to 1982 had been answered by GM with "false and misleading statements" (*The New York Times*, 4 August 1983, A1, and 15 August 1983, A17). Although his later activities may make John DeLorean's account suspect, he did have an insider's view of GM as head of Pontiac, Chevrolet, and finally the entire GM Car and Truck Group, and his comments on the Corvair paint a similar picture (Wright 1979, 63–67; see also Herman 1981, 260–64).

porate enterprises, they would need some regulation by the state. For that very reason, I assumed earlier that enterprises would operate within limits set by such democratically imposed laws, rules, and regulations as the public holds necessary.

Nonetheless, two important differences would help to foster greater moral responsibility. First, self-governing enterprises would in principle eliminate, and surely would in practice vastly reduce, the adversarial and antagonistic relations between employers and employees that foster moral irresponsibility on both sides. Every employee would have a stake in the firm's welfare; actions adverse to the performance of the firm would be hurtful to all. Second, being far more numerous and closer to the average citizen than managers and owners, employees would be more representative of consumers and citizens. Whereas top managers are a minuscule proportion of the public and can more easily escape or absorb the social costs their decisions generate, employees are much larger and more representative part of the public, as consumers, residents, and citizens. They are therefore much more likely than managers to bear some of the adverse consequence of their decisions.

To repeat, a system of relatively autonomous enterprises would require controls external to the enterprise, both by markets and prices and by democratically imposed laws and regulations. Both forms of external control finally depend for their existence and effectiveness on public support. I see no reason why public support for these controls would be less in a system of self-governing enterprises than they are under corporate capitalism.

Effects on political equality.   In the preceding chapter I referred to the classical republican problem of distributing power and property: If property is distributed in a highly unequal fashion, a conflict will tend to arise between democracy and property rights. The obvious republican solution was to ensure, somehow, that property be distributed more or less evenly. In the United States, the ideology of agrarian democratic republicanism promised a unique form of that solution: Factors largely external to the political process—principally a vast supply of cheap land—would ensure that economic resources would be so widely diffused as to promote and sustain a satisfactory approximation to political equality.

As it turned out, however, this solution proved to be historically ephemeral. The new social and economic order that gradually replaced the American agrarian society in the course of the nineteenth century did not spontaneously generate the equality of condition so sharply emphasized by Tocqueville as a fundamental characteristic of American agrarian society. On the contrary, the new order produced enormous differences in wealth, income, status, and power. Clearly a solution to the classical republican problem could no longer depend on the accidental existence of a factor, like land, that was mainly exogenous to the political process. In a system where wealth and income were allocated unequally through the institutions of market-oriented capitalism, to maintain a distribution of political resources favorable to political equality would require that economic resources be either somehow divorced from political life (which the republican tradition assumed was impossible), or else massively reallocated, presumably by the state. Either solution would have generated a perpetual conflict between those who benefited most from the initial distribution and the political forces favoring political equality. Even if a sufficiently powerful and stable coalition of egalitarian forces to execute either policy had developed, political life would have been persistently polarized. In any case, no such coalition ever developed and neither policy was ever executed.

Moreover, it is an open question whether business will turn in a satisfactory performance in a privately owned, market-oriented economy if wealth and income are massively redistributed. Charles E. Lindblom has attributed a "privileged position" to business by virtue of its need for inducements (Lindblom 1977, 170ff.). By privileged, as I understand him, he means that in order to persuade investors and managers in privately owned business firms to perform satisfactorily, a society must provide them with strong inducements in the form of large financial rewards. But a structure of rewards substantial enough to persuade investors and managers to perform their social functions satisfactorily will create a highly inegalitarian distribution of wealth and income. In the United States the ideological defense of economic inegalitarianism came to be known during the late nineteenth century as the Gospel of Wealth and in this century as the "trickle down" theory. Although exaggerated claims are often made for the social contributions of business that result from adhering to the Gospel of Wealth, the notion has a discomforting element of validity. Corporate capitalism does seem to require allocating great financial rewards to property owners. In the United States, given the concentration of ownership, these rewards accrue mainly to a small minority of investors.[5] As a consequence, American society seems to require economic inequalities more extreme than Jefferson could ever have thought possible or permissible among a people with democratic aspirations.

5. In 1969, 1.3 percent of the adult U.S. population, and 5.6 percent of all stockholders, owned 53.3 percent of all corporate stock (Smith, Franklin, and Wion 1973, table 5). And "approximately 5 percent of all families receive about 40 percent of dividend, interest, rent, and royalty incomes, while the lowest two-thirds of families receive less than 20 percent of income of this type" (Schnitzer 1974, 38). Peter Drucker argues, however, that data like these overstate the concentration of wealth and income from wealth because they do not take into account the rapid expansion since 1950, when GM inaugurated a pension fund for its workers, of pension funds that invest in equities and thus acquire ownership of firms. He estimates that in 1974, pension funds owned about 30 percent of the total value of the stocks of all companies traded on the stock market (and predicts that by 1985 their share will be 50 percent). If the pension plans of the self-employed (Keogh Plans), Individual Retirement Accounts (IRAs), and government employees are added, "this amounts to a minimum of 50 percent and a 'most probable' of 65 to 70 percent of equity ownership by the pension funds within the next ten or fifteen years" (Drucker 1976, 12 and 16).

Wishing to escape these difficulties, we might search for a socioeconomic structure that would itself tend to generate a greater equality of condition, what I referred to in Chapter 2 as a self-regulating egalitarian order. With such an order, the tendency toward equality would not have to be sustained over the opposition of a powerful, well-entrenched minority in a polarized national conflict. Instead it would be produced spontaneously by a socioeconomic structure supported by a widespread consensus.

Would a system of self-governing enterprises constitute a self-regulating egalitarian order? Obviously not. Although it is impossible to say precisely how far such a system, operating autonomously without externally imposed reallocations (e.g., by taxes and transfer payments), would verge toward equality in wealth, income, and other resources, it is clear that inequality would tend to arise both *within* firms and *among* firms. In self-governing enterprises, the members themselves would decide on the principles according to which wages, salaries, and surplus were to be distributed among the members. Their choice of internal distributive principles would depend on factors that are very far from predictable, including their implicit and explicit beliefs about fairness, which in turn would be influenced by tradition, the prevailing culture, ideology, religion, and the like; and on the extent to which they would find it desirable or necessary to adjust wages and salaries to the supply of and demand for various skills. Although theorists and ideologues may often set forth quite definite views as to the principles of distribution that workers *ought* to choose, it is flatly impossible to predict which they *would* choose.

It is reasonable to suppose, however, that members of self-governing enterprises would maintain wage and salary differentials within their firms at much lower ratios than the ten-to-one, or even twenty-to-one, that exist in American firms. They would also be less likely to provide top executives with the per-quisites that increase the differentials even further, in some cases to 100-to-1: bonuses, stock-options, re-tirement benefits, and salary guarantees—"golden parachutes"—should they lose their jobs after a take-over.[6] Finally, inequalities in income and wealth would be reduced still more because the surplus of a self-governing firm would be shared among all its members, within whatever limits might be established

6. The argument that high compensation is a reward for excep-tional performance does not hold water. A *Fortune* study of 140 large companies shows little or no correlation between the com-pensation of the chief executive and performance as measured by return on stockholders' equity. In the ten industries surveyed, only one—metal manufacturing—revealed "much correlation between pay and performance." By contrast "the correlation be-tween size [of firm] and pay, though by no means perfect, is relatively high, and superior to any other single pay correlation tested" (Loomis 1982, 44 and 49). A 1982 survey by *The Econo-mist* of the 100 biggest companies in Britain led to similar conclu-sions: "There is still no obvious connection between bosses' sala-ries and the performance of the companies they run in most of British industry. The size of a company is often a better guide to salaries at the top" (*The Economist*, 18 September 1982, 75ff.).

through the democratic process in the government of the state.

If we turn from speculation to actual practice we find that although producer cooperatives have adopted a variety of distributive principles, in few cases (if any) do the differences approach those in private firms. To be sure, not many producer cooperatives have followed the example of the Israeli kibbutzim in their adherence to a principle of complete equality (whether lot-regarding or need-regarding) in the distribution of material and cultural resources among the members. And even the kibbutzim have departed from strict equality in the wages they pay to hired workers, who are not members. Although the plywood cooperative of the Pacific Northwest adopted a principle of equal pay and an equal share in the surplus for all members, their hired managers, who are not members, are paid competitive salaries—which are significantly higher than the payments to the members. The worker-managed Mondragon cooperatives in Spain have sought from the beginning to "[limit] differentials from exceeding a three-to-one range between highest and lowest earnings." In practice, that ratio is not fully maintained, though violations are quite modest: for 98 percent of the members the difference in earnings does not exceed about 4-to-1, and for 90 percent about 2.8-to-1. Of equal significance, the spread in the distribution of wealth among members is also quite narrow (Thomas and Logan 1982, 11, 143–45, 159). Thus the conclusion seems warranted that within self-governing enterprises the distribution of income and wealth would be significantly less unequal than it will be in a system of corporate capitalism—as in American firms, for example.[7]

But inequalities will also arise between firms. Differences in markets, changing demand, varying ratios of capital to labor, regional differences in labor supply, and many other factors will create differences in the revenues available to self-governing firms and industries for distribution to their members.[8]

Conclusion

A system of self-governing enterprises could not be relied on, then, to create a completely self-regulating

7. In "the largest diversified machinery producer in Yugoslavia, it was a skilled worker who, in 1968, made the highest pay—2,993 dinars per month—more than the general director" (Dirlam and Plummer 1973, 66).

8. Yugoslavia provides plenty of evidence. "Interskill differences within single enterprises, legitimized under the distribution according to work principle, proved less of an ideological problem than interindustry differentials" (Comisso 1979, 108; see also her discussion of the "inequalities issue," 94–115). And Joel B. Dirlam remarks: "An examination of the Yugoslav wage system in 1973 concluded that wage levels varied among industries largely in conformity with average productivity, which in turn could be explained by the capital endowment of the industry. Moreover, those industries with high capital/labor ratios tended to enjoy high wages" (Dirlam 1979, 347). Saul Estrin, who analyzed Yugoslav "intersectoral and interfirm income differences from 1956 to 1974," found large interfirm income differences within each sector. In the entire industrial sector "between 10 and 14 percent of firm-size groups paid on average, less than 50 percent or more than 200 percent of the industrial mean" (Estrin and Bartlett

egalitarian order. Although the magnitude cannot be accurately forecast, interfirm and intrafirm differentials would create differences in personal resources that conceivably might be large enough to have adverse effects both on political equality and on our standards of fairness. To be sure, because the citizen-members of firms would themselves decide on the principles according to which intrafirm differences were determined, presumably intrafirm differences would tend to satisfy their standards. But to the extent that interfirm differences were caused by factors other than effort and skill—by history, geography, society, and luck—results might well seem unfair. Thus to prevent an excessive erosion of political equality and distributive justice, we might want to alter the initial distribution of personal resources generated by the enterprises (by taxes and transfers, for example), or to regulate the effects (for example, by limiting the use of money in politics), or to do both.

The task of regulation and redistribution would be much easier, however, than in a system of corporate capitalism. For one, the initial distribution generated by the enterprises would be much less unequal. Thus while not completely self-regulating, such a system would come far closer than corporate capitalism to the classical republican solution mentioned in Chapter 2, that is, a wide diffusion of economic resources among citizens.

1982, 95). In 1968, the average personal income of workers in the textile industry was one-third that of workers in design and less than 40 percent of workers in maritime transport (Dirlam and Plummer 1973, table 4-1).

Moreover, full and equal citizenship in economic enterprises would greatly reduce the adversarial and conflictive relationships within firms, and indirectly in society and politics at large. In the corporate system, managers are legally bound to act and typically do act on the view that the interests of employees are secondary to the interests of owners. In a system of self-management, in contrast, managers chosen directly or indirectly by workers would give priority to the interests of the citizen-members. In the one theoretical model, managers act so as to maximize net returns to stockholders; in the other, they act to maximize net returns per capita to the citizen-members. Thus the adversarial and conflictive relations inherent to the very structure of the private firm would be greatly attenuated (indeed eliminated in the theoretical model) in self-governing enterprises.

The internally conflictive relations of private enterprise also spill over to conflicts about redistributive policies and the regulation of money in politics. As a small minority of the most privileged members of society, American businessmen—like Kent, Story, and Leigh, who feared that democracy would destroy property—tend to harbor a deep distrust of political equality, majority rule, Congress, and the institutions of democratic government generally (cf. Silk and Vogel 1976, 189–201). Like their predecessors, they seek to use their superior resources—in money, organization, status, and access—to protect their possession of and opportunities to acquire these superior resources. It is hardly surprising, therefore, that reform efforts directed toward redistributive policies and the effective regulation of money in politics meet with so little success in the United States.

A system of self-governing enterprises would not, of course, eliminate conflicting interests, goals, perspectives, and ideologies among citizens. But it would tend to reduce the conflict of interests, give all citizens a more nearly equal stake in maintaining political equality and democratic institutions in the government of the state, and facilitate the development of a stronger consensus on standards of fairness.

4

The Right to Democracy Within Firms

Although political theorists who favor worker participation have often emphasized its potentialities for
democratic character and its beneficial effects on democracy in the government of the state, a stronger
justification, one with a more Kantian flavor, seems
to me to rest on a different argument: *If* democracy is
justified in governing the state, then it must *also* be
justified in governing economic enterprises; and to
say that it is *not* justified in governing economic enterprises is to imply that it is not justified in governing the state.

I can readily imagine three objections to this
argument:

1. A system of self-governing enterprises would
violate a superior right to property.
2. The assumptions in Chapter 2 that justify the
democratic process do not apply to an economic enterprise because decisions in economic enterprises are
not *binding* in the same sense as decisions made and
enforced by the government of a state. Furthermore,

because employees are generally not as well qualified as others to run a company, the principle of equality does not hold, and the argument for the democratic process falls. Whereas, on the contrary, a government by the best qualified, that is, a system of guardianship or meritocracy, is justified by the marked differences in competence. Rule by corporate managers, it might be argued, is such a system.

3. A tendency toward oligarchy, hierarchy, or domination operates so strongly in economic enterprises that democracy would prove to be a sham in any case. Thus the effort to inaugurate the democratic process within firms is essentially a waste of time.

In this chapter, I address these objections in turn.

Property Rights

As to property rights, transferring control over the decisions of a firm to its employees, it might be objected, would violate the right of owners to use their property as they choose. If, however, this objection assumes that people have an inherent right to establish and maintain economic enterprises in their present corporate form, and that any attempt to replace this form with another would violate that right, then the argument runs headlong into all the difficulties described in Chapter 2. Moreover, if a right to property is understood in its fundamental moral sense as a right to acquire the personal resources necessary to political liberty and a decent existence, then self-governing enterprises would surely not, on balance, diminish the capacity of citizens to exercise that right; in all likelihood they would greatly strengthen it. Even if property rights are construed in a narrower, more legalistic sense, the way in which a self-governing enterprise is owned need not *necessarily* violate such a right. As we shall see, it could entail a *shift* of ownership from stockholders to employees.

Are Decisions Binding?

However, can the assumptions set out in Chapter 2 as justifying the democratic process reasonably be applied to economic enterprises? For example, do economic enterprises make decisions that are *binding* on workers in the same way that the government of the state makes decisions that citizens are compelled to obey? After all, laws made by the government of a state can be enforced by physical coercion, if need be. In a democratic state, a minority opposed to a law is nevertheless compelled to obey it. But a firm, it might be said, is nothing more than a sort of market within which people engage in voluntary individual exchanges: workers voluntarily exchange their labor in return for wages paid by the employer. Decisions made by the government of a firm and by the government of the state, however, are in some crucial respects more similar than this classical liberal interpretation allows for. Like the government of the state, the government of a firm makes decisions that apply uniformly to all workers or a category of workers:

decisions governing the place of work, time of work, product of work, minimally acceptable rate of work, equipment to be used at work, number of workers, number (and identity) of workers laid off in slack times—or whether the plant is to be shut down and there will be no work at all. These decisions are enforced by sanctions, including the ultimate sanction of firing.

Have I now understated the difference? Unlike citizens of a state, one might object, workers are not *compelled* to obey managerial decisions; their decision to do so is voluntary. Because a worker may choose to obey the management or not, because he is free to leave the firm if he prefers not to obey, and because he cannot be punished by management for leaving, some would argue that his decision to obey is perfectly free of all compulsion.

But an objection along these lines exaggerates the differences between a worker's subjection to decisions made by the government of a firm and a citizen's subjection to decisions made by the government of the state. Take a local government. A citizen who does not like a local ordinance is also "free" to move to another community. Indeed, if a citizen does not want to obey her country's laws, she is "free"—at least in all democratic countries—to leave her country. Now if a citizen were perfectly free to leave, then citizenship would be wholly voluntary; for if a citizen found "voice" unsatisfactory, she could freely opt for "exit." But is not "exit" (or exile) often so costly, in every sense, that membership is for all practical purposes compulsory—whether it requires one to leave a country, a municipality, or a firm? If so, then the government of a firm looks rather more like the government of a state than we are habitually inclined to believe: because exit is so costly, membership in a firm is not significantly more voluntary or less compulsory than citizenship in a municipality or perhaps even in a country.

In fact, citizenship in a democratic state is in one respect more voluntary than employment in a firm. Within a democratic country, citizens may ordinarily leave one municipality and automatically retain or quickly acquire full rights of citizenship in another. Yet even though the decisions of firms, like the decisions of a state, can be enforced by severe sanctions (firing), unlike a citizen of a democratic state, one who leaves a firm has no right to "citizenship" (that is, employment) in another.

Like a state, then, a firm can also be viewed as a political system in which relations of power exist between governments and the governed. If so, is it not appropriate to insist that the relationship between governors and governed should satisfy the criteria of the democratic process—as we properly insist in the domain of the state?

Let the firm be considered a political system, one might now agree. Within this political system, however, cannot the rights of workers be adequately protected by labor unions? But this objection not only fails to meet the problem of nonunion workers (who in the United States compose about 80 percent of the workforce); it also implicitly recognizes that in order to protect some fundamental right or interest, workers are entitled to—have a right to—at least *some* democratic controls. What, then, is the nature and scope of this right or interest? To say that its scope is limited by an equally or more fundamental right to property runs afoul of our earlier analysis. On what grounds, therefore, must the employees' *right* to democratic controls be restricted to the conventional (but by no means well-defined) limits of trade unions? Is this not precisely the question at issue: Do workers have a fundamental right to self-government in their economic enterprises? If they do have such a right, then is it not obvious that, however essential conventional trade unions may be in reducing the impact of authoritarian rule in the government of a firm,[1] an ordinary firm, even with a trade union, still falls very far short of satisfying the criteria of the democratic process?

Does the Strong Principle of Equality Hold?

In Chapter 2, I argued that the democratic process is justified by the strong principle of equality. But if the strong principle does not apply to business firms, then the case for self-governing enterprises is seriously, perhaps fatally, damaged, while the case for rule by the best qualified—the "guardians," to use

1. Ellerman contends that even in self-governing enterprises, trade unions would be important, particularly in performing the functions of a "loyal opposition" (Ellerman, "The Union as the Legitimate Opposition," n.d.).

Plato's term—is correspondingly strengthened. The government of large American corporations, I suggested earlier, could be seen as a form of guardianship. Although managers are nominally selected by a board of directors, which in turn is nominally chosen by and legally accountable to stockholders, in reality new managers are typically co-opted by existing management which also, in practice, chooses and controls its own board of directors (Herman 1981). Guardianship has also been the ideal of many socialists, particularly the Fabians. In this view the managers of state-owned enterprises were to be chosen by state officials, to whom the top managers were to be ultimately responsible. In most countries, in fact, nationalized industries are governed by some such scheme. One could easily dream up still other meritocratic alternatives.

Thus in theory and practice both corporate capitalism and bureaucratic socialism have rejected the strong principle of equality for economic enterprises; explicitly or by implication they uphold guardianship. Because of the overwhelming weight of existing institutions and ideologies, probably most people, including many thoughtful people, will find it hard to believe that employees are qualified to govern the enterprises in which they work. However, in considering whether the strong principle of equality holds for business firms, it is important to keep two points in mind. First, while we may reasonably compare the ideal or theoretically possible performance of one system with the ideal or theoretical performance of another, we cannot reasonably compare the actual performance of one with the ideal performance of another. Although a good deal of the discussion of self-governing enterprises that follows is necessarily conjectural, my aim is to compare the probable performance of self-governing enterprises with the actual performance of their current principal alternative, the modern privately owned corporation.

Second, as we saw in Chapter 2, the strong principle of equality does not require that citizens be equally competent in every respect. It is sufficient to believe that citizens are qualified enough to decide which matters do or do not require binding collective decisions (e.g., which matters require general rules); of those that do require binding collective decisions, citizens are competent to decide whether they are themselves sufficiently qualified to make the decisions collectively through the democratic process; and on matters they do not feel competent to decide for themselves, they are qualified to set the terms on which they will delegate these decisions to others.

Except in exceedingly small firms, employees would surely choose to delegate some decisions to managers. In larger firms, they would no doubt elect a governing board or council, which in the typical case would probably be delegated the authority to select and remove the top executives. Except in very large enterprises, the employees might constitute an assembly for "legislative" purposes—to make decisions on such matters as the workers choose to decide, to delegate matters they prefer not to decide directly, and to review decisions on matters they had previously delegated as well as the conduct of the board and the managers in other ways. In giant firms, where an assembly would suffer all the infirmities of direct democracy on an excessively large scale, a representative government would have to be created.

Given the passivity of stockholders in a typical firm, their utter dependency on information supplied by management, and the extraordinary difficulties of contesting a managerial decision, it seems to me hardly open to doubt that employees are on the whole as well qualified to run their firms as are stockholders, and probably on average a good deal more. But of course that is not really the issue, given the separation of ownership from control that Adolf Berle and Gardiner Means called attention to in 1932 in *The Modern Corporation and Private Property*. A recent and much more systematic study reports that 64 percent of the 200 largest nonfinancial American corporations are controlled by inside management and another 17 percent by inside management with an outside board, or altogether 81 percent of the total, with 84 percent of the assets and 82 percent of the sales (Herman 1981, table 3.1). Although the percentage of management-controlled firms might be less among smaller firms, the question remains whether workers are as qualified to govern economic enterprises as managers who gain their position by co-option—thus producing a sort of co-optive guardianship.

This question raises many of the familiar and ancient issues of democracy versus guardianship, including the grounds for believing that the putative guardians possess superior knowledge about what is best for the collectivity, and also superior virtue—the will or predisposition to seek that good. It is important therefore to distinguish knowledge about the *ends* the enterprise should seek from technical knowledge about the best *means* for achieving those ends. As to ends, the argument might be made that self-governing enterprises would produce lower rates of savings, investment, growth, and employment than the society might rationally (or at least reasonably) prefer. As to means, it might be contended that self-governing enterprises would be less likely to supply qualified management and for this and other reasons would be less efficient than stockholder-owned firms like American corporations.

Ends: Savings, investment, growth, and employment. How then would a system of self-governing enterprises affect savings, investment, employment, and growth? For example, would workers vote to allocate so much of enterprise earnings to wages that they would sacrifice investment in new machinery and future efficiencies? Would firms run democratically by their employees be more shortsighted than firms run hierarchically by managers? American corporate managers are frequently criticized nowadays for an excessive emphasis on short-run as against long-run returns (e.g., Bluestone 1980, 52). Would self-governing enterprises accentuate the sacrifice of deferred to immediate benefits, to the disadvantage and contrary to the collective preferences of their society? If so, would not the particular interests of workers in an enterprise conflict with the general interest?

Purely theoretical analysis by economists, whether critics or advocates of worker-managed firms, is ultimately inconclusive. Advocates of self-management agree that in contrast to conventional firms in which managers seek to maximize total profit for share-holders, the worker-members of self-governing firms would seek to maximize the per capita income of the members.[2] In view of this, some critics reason, members would have no incentive to expand savings, production, employment, or investment unless the effect were to increase their own per capita earnings; and they would have a definite incentive not to do so if they expected that by doing so they would reduce their own earnings. These critics therefore conclude that in some situations in which a conventional firm would expand in order to increase returns to share-holders, worker-managed firms would not.[3]

2. For example, see Vanek 1970, 2–3; Jay 1980, 17.

3. These and other theoretical arguments are summarized and evaluated by Estrin and Barrett (1982); for a well-known early theoretical formulation see Ward (1957, 1958, 1967). One theoretical argument can be illustrated as follows. Assume a firm with 100 members, a daily output of 100 units—each selling at $200 a unit, and costs for nonlabor inputs (equipment, buildings, materials, etc.) of $150 a unit. The total return available for distribution to workers is $5,000, or $50 per member. Assume that by doubling the workforce (and thus membership), output would rise to 150 units at the same unit cost. Although the amount available for distribution to members would rise to $7,500, the share of each member would fall to $37.50. Thus (unless they were altruists) the members would be unwilling to expand their firm's employment and membership. If, however, they were legally permitted to, they might try to hire additional workers at a wage low enough to protect their own current earnings; in our example, such a wage would have to be less than $25. A specific case of this kind was the system of worker-controlled cooperatives in Peru (Stepan 1978, 216ff.).

Advocates of self-governing firms reply that in an economy of self-governing firms, the problem of employment is theoretically distinguishable from the problem of investment and growth. In the theoretical scenario just sketched out, expanding employment is a problem only at the level of the individual firm. At the level of the economy, however, it would be dealt with by ensuring ease of entry for new firms. If unemployment existed and enterprises failed to respond to rising demand for their product by expanding employment, new firms would do so; hence both investment and employment would increase. As to investment, except in the circumstances just described, members of a self-managed enterprise would have strong incentives to invest, and thus to save, whenever by doing so they would increase the surplus available for distribution to themselves (cf. Jay 1980, 17–27; Schweikart 1980, 73–74, 103–36).

In the real world, however, these comparisons between theoretical models do not take us very far. As Peter Jay remarks:

So far we have been comparing the rational investment behavior of workers' cooperatives with the rational behavior of idealized capital enterprises working according to textbook optimization. If we actually lived in the latter world, we would hardly be considering the problem discussed in this paper at all.

(*Jay, 20*)

Turning then to the domain of practical judgment, it seems likely that in the real world, self-governing

enterprises might stimulate as much savings, investment, and growth as American corporate enterprises
have done, and perhaps more, because workers typically stand to incur severe losses from the decline of a
firm. If we permit ourselves to violate the unenforce-
able injunction of some welfare economists against
interpersonal comparisons, we can hardly deny that
the losses incurred by workers from the decline of a
firm are normally even greater than those investors
suffer; for it is ordinarily much easier and less costly
in human terms for a well-heeled investor to switch
in and out of the securities market than for a worker
to switch in and out of the job market. A moderately
foresightful worker would therefore be as greatly
concerned with long-run efficiencies as a rational investor or a rational manager, and perhaps more so.

This conjecture is supported by at least some cases
in which, given the opportunity, workers have made
significant short-term sacrifices in wages and benefits
in order to keep their firm from collapsing. They did
so, for example, at both Chrysler Corporation and
the Rath Packing Company. And when workers own
the company their incentive to sacrifice in order to
save it is all the stronger. As a worker in one of the
plywood co-ops put it, "If things get bad we'll all
take a pay cut. You don't want to milk the cow, because if you milk the cow, there's nothing left. And
we lose the company" (Zwerdling 1980, 101).

Perhaps an even more relevant example is that of
Mondragon, a complex of more than 80 worker co-
operatives in Spain. During a period in which the
Spanish economy was expanding generally, the sales

of the Mondragon cooperatives grew at an impressive rate, averaging 8.5 percent from 1970 to 1979. Their market share increased from less than 1 percent in 1960 to over 10 percent in 1976. The percentage of gross value added through investment by the cooperatives between 1971 and 1979 averaged 36 percent, nearly four times the average rate of industry in the heavily industrialized Basque province in which Mondragon is located (Thomas and Logan 1982, 100–105). Moreover, when a recession in the Spanish economy led to declining profits in 1981, "investment [was] squeezed, but the workers [were] prepared to make sacrifices to keep their jobs, digging into their own pockets to keep the balance sheets in shape" (*The Economist*, 31 October 1981, 84). Members chose to contribute more capital rather than cut their wages. Thus the members of one co-op voted to increase their individual capital contributions by amounts that ranged from $570 to $1,700, depending on wage level. Nor have the self-managed enterprises of Yugoslavia on the whole followed the theoretical model advanced by critics of self-management.[4] Though the causes are complex, with some exceptions they have not sacrificed investment to current

4. Dirlam and Plummer comment that the self-managed enterprises "do not (contrary to Ward's model) appear to reduce output when prices rise, but they set their prices to cover costs, including fixed cost . . . and *akontacija* wage—if they can obtain it. They may try to cut employment to improve the firm's financial position, but only in circumstances where private owners would probably follow the same course" (1973, 57). The *akontacija* is in effect a monthly wage, as distinct from a periodic (usually annual) bonus *visak* allocated in successful firms from the surplus over planned costs.

income but, on the contrary, have maintained very high levels of investment.[5]

A final observation on the problem of savings, investment, employment, and growth: The introduction of self-governing enterprises *could* be accompanied by the creation of new investment funds operating under democratic control. Although a system of self-governing enterprises of the kind suggested in this chapter differs in crucial ways from the proposals for wage-earner funds advanced by the Swedish Social Democratic party, that proposal is relevant because of its emphasis on funds for investment. Often called the Meidner Plan after its author, Rudolf Meidner, who developed it with his colleagues in the research bureau of the national trade union organization or LO (Meidner 1978), the proposal was

5. According to one estimate, until recently Yugoslav investment may have run as high as 35 to 40 percent of the national income (Sirc, in Clayre 1980, 166 and 194; see also Rusinow 1977, 127). However, this extraordinarily high rate was at least partly attributable to rates on long-term loans that kept the real interest rate low or negative; the failure to enforce penalties for nonpayment of loans (including short-term loans that bear higher rates); the practical absence of bankruptcy as a deterrent; and the "political" nature of many loans (Estrin and Bartlett 1982, 90–93; Dirlam and Plummer 1973, 183). Many Yugoslav economists concluded that the rate of investment was excessive, and exacted too high a cost in consumption. In the mid 1960s, a debate on this question (and others) erupted between "conservatives" who blamed market forces and "liberals" who saw a need for strengthening market forces even more (Rusinow 1977, 126ff.). Despite frequent reforms in the system of banking and credit, by 1983 the economy was in deep recession, and the 1983 economic development plan called for a cut of 20 percent in public investment (*The New York Times*, 9 January 1983, 6).

adopted by the LO in 1976 and, in altered form, by the Social Democrats in 1978. As revised by 1980, the proposal would require the largest firms—altogether about 200 companies—to set aside each year 20 percent of their profits in the form of "wage-earner shares" that would carry voting rights. As a result, ownership of these firms would gradually pass to the employees. At a 10 percent rate of profit, for example, wage earners would gain majority ownership in about thirty-five years.

However, the wage-earner shares would not belong to individual workers, as they do in employee stock ownership plans, nor to the workers of an enterprise collectively. Instead, the shares and therefore the voting rights would be transferred to various national and regional funds, which would be governed by representatives elected by wage-earners—*all* wage-earners, it should be added, not only those employed by the 200 or so contributing firms. A firm's employees would never control more than 20 percent of the voting rights in their own firm, whereas an increasingly larger share would accrue to one of the representative bodies.[6] With a powerful, unified, and

6. In an attempt to meet objections to the original Meidner plan, by 1980 the plan had become quite complex. The description given here is partly drawn from an unpublished paper by Peter Swenson, "Socialism on the Democratic Agenda: The Swedish Proposal for Labor Ownership and Control in Industry" (1980). I want to express my appreciation to Peter Swenson for allowing me to use the information in his paper. I have also profited from a paper by Bo Gustafsson, "Co-determination and Wage Earners' Funds, the Swedish Experience" delivered at a conference on The Limits of Democracy, Perugia, 26–28 April 1983.

inclusive trade union organization and a history of success in using centralized national bargaining to equalize wages and a centralized government to socialize incomes, the Swedish labor movement and the Social Democratic party are disposed to favor a more centralized solution than the system I am suggesting. The important point, however, is that the funds are intended not only to provide "economic democracy" but also to ensure a greater supply of capital for investment.[7]

Much closer to the idea of self-governing enterprises described here is a proposal introduced in Parliament by the Danish Social Democratic party in 1973 (Ministry of Labour 1973). The proceeds of a payroll tax covering most Danish firms (about 25,000) would be divided, in effect, in two parts. One part—the smaller—would go to a national investment and dividend fund that would be used both to strengthen Danish investment and to provide a social dividend to Danish workers. Virtually every worker would receive certificates from the fund in an amount proportional to the number of years worked but not to the employee's wage or salary. The certificates would be nonnegotiable, but an employee would have the right to withdraw the value of his certificates after seven years or at age 67; upon death their value would be paid to the employee's estate. The other and larger part of the proceeds from the payroll tax would re-

7. Although the Social Democrats muted their support in the 1982 elections, in 1983 they undertook to implement the plan by legislation, despite massive and clamorous opposition from businessmen and some white-collar workers.

main in the firm as share capital owned collectively by the employees, who would vote as enterprise-citizens, that is, one person, one vote. The employees' share of capital, however, and thus of voting rights, would not be permitted to increase beyond 50 percent—presumably a provision to reassure private investors. Like the Meidner Plan in Sweden, the Danish proposal is intended to achieve several purposes: greater equalization of wealth, more democratic control of the economy, and, definitely not least in importance, a steady supply of funds for investment.

Thus it is not inconceivable that workers might enter into a social contract that would require them to provide funds for investment, drawn from payrolls, in return for greater control over the government of economic enterprises. If self-governing enterprises proved to be better matched to the incentives of workers than hierarchically run firms, and thus more efficient, a system of self-governing enterprises might be a prescription for economic growth that would surpass even Japan's success—and leave recent American performance far behind.

Means: Managerial skills.   A disastrous assumption of revolutionaries, exhibited with stunning naivete in Lenin's *State and Revolution*, is that managerial skills are of trivial importance, or will arise spontaneously, or will be more than compensated for by revolutionary enthusiasm. The historical record relieves one of all need to demonstrate the foolishness of such an assumption. The question is obviously not whether self-governing enterprises would need managerial abilities, but whether workers and their representatives would select and oversee managers less competently than is now the case in American corporations, which are largely controlled by managers whose decisions are rarely open to serious challenge, except when disaster strikes, and not always even then (Herman 1981). If a system of self-governing enterprises were established it would be wise to provide much wider opportunities than now exist in any country for employees to learn some of the tools and skills of modern management. One source of the Mondragon cooperatives' success lies in the prominence they have assigned to education, including technical education at advanced professional levels. As a result, they have developed their own managers (Thomas and Logan, 42–74). In the United States, at least, a significant proportion of both blue- and white-collar workers, often the more ambitious and aggressive among them, aspire to supervisory and managerial positions but lack the essential skills (see, e.g., Witte 1980). Efficiency and economic growth flow from investments in human capital every bit as much as from financial capital, and probably more (cf. Denison 1974). A system of self-governing enterprises would be likely to heighten—not diminish—efforts to improve a country's human capital.

If in the meanwhile skilled managers are in short supply, self-governing enterprises will have to compete for their services, as does Puget Sound Plywood, a worker-owned cooperative. The president and members of the board of trustees are elected by and from the members, who all receive the same pay.

However, the president and board in turn select a general manager from outside the membership "because he can command pay that is far in excess of what he could realize as a shareholder [i.e., as a worker-member]. . . . The qualifications for being a general manager are not what one would normally gain from working in a plywood mill. So we usually employ the best person we can find in the industry" (Bennett 1979, 81–82, 85).

Means: Efficiency.   Unless self-governing enterprises were less competent in recruiting skilled managers, they should be no less efficient in a narrow sense than American corporations at present. And unless they were more likely to evade the external controls of competition and regulation, they should not be less efficient in a broader sense. I have suggested why it is reasonable to expect neither of these deficiencies to occur.

Yet if self-governing enterprises can be as efficient as orthodox firms, why have they so often failed? As everyone familiar with American and British labor history knows, the late nineteenth century saw waves of short-lived producer cooperatives in Britain and in the United States. Their quick demise convinced trade union leaders that in a capitalist economy unionism and collective bargaining held out a much more realistic promise of gains for workers than producer cooperatives. In both countries, and in Europe as well, labor and socialist movements largely abandoned producer cooperatives as a major short-run objective. Most academic observers, including labor economists and social historians, concluded that the labor-managed firm was a rejected and forlorn utopian idea irrelevant to a modern economy (e.g., Commons et al. 1936, 2:488).

In recent years, however, a number of factors have brought about a reassessment of the relevance of the older experience (cf. Jones and Svejnar 1982, 4–6). These include the highly unsatisfactory performance of both corporate capitalism and bureaucratic socialism, whose failings have stimulated a search for a third alternative; the introduction and survival—despite severe difficulties—of self-management in Yugoslavia; some stunning successes, such as the U.S. plywood cooperatives and the Mondragon group; formal economic analysis showing how a labor-managed market economy would theoretically satisfy efficiency criteria (Vanek 1970); growing awareness of the need to reduce the hierarchical structure of the workplace and increase participation by workers in order to increase productivity; and the seeming success of many new arrangements for worker participation, control, or ownership in Europe and the United States.

In sum, it has become clear that many failed labor-managed firms had been doomed not by inherent weaknesses but by remediable ones, such as shortages of credit, capital, and managerial skills. Moreover, in the past, producer cooperatives have usually been organized in the worst possible circumstances, when employees desperately attempt to rescue a collapsing company by taking it over—often during a recession. It is hardly surprising that workers may fail to save a firm after management has already failed. What is surprising is that workers' cooperatives have sometimes succeeded where private management has failed. For example, it was from the failure of privately owned companies that some of the plywood co-ops started (Berman 1982, 63).

I have also mentioned the Mondragon producer cooperatives in Spain as an example of success. They include their nation's largest manufacturer of machine tools as well as one of its largest refrigerator manufacturers. During a period of a falling Spanish economy and rising unemployment, between 1977 and 1981, employment in the Mondragon co-ops increased from 15,700 to about 18,500 (Zwerdling 1980, 154ff. and *The Economist*, 31 October 1981, 84). Unless they are denied access to credit—the Mondragon complex has its own bank (Thomas and Logan, 75–95)—self-governing enterprises have a greater resiliency than American corporations. For in times of stringency when an orthodox private firm would lay off workers or shut down, the members of a self-governing enterprise can decide to reduce their wages, curtail their share of the surplus, if any, or even contribute additional capital funds, as at Mondragon. As these and other cases show, self-governing enterprises are likely to tap the creativity, energies, and loyalties of workers to an extent that stockholder-owned corporations probably never can, even with profit-sharing schemes (cf. Melman 1958).

Although rigorous comparisons of the relative efficiencies of labor-managed and conventional corporations are difficult and still fairly uncommon, the best analysis (Jones and Svejnar 1982) of a broad range of experiences in a number of different countries appears to support these conclusions: participation by workers in decision-making rarely leads to a decline of productivity; far more often it either has no effect or results in an increase in productivity (see also Simmons and Mares 1983, 285–93).

How Much Internal Democracy?

Often the effects of more democratic corporate structures have been greatly exaggerated by both advocates and opponents. Yet just as the democratization of the authoritarian structures of centralized monarchies and modern dictatorships has transformed relations of authority and power in the government of states, so there is every reason to believe that the democratization of the government of modern corporations would profoundly alter relations of authority and power in economic enterprises. Relationships of governors to governed of a sort that Americans have insisted on for two hundred years in the public governments of the state would be extended to the hitherto private governments in the economy.

If too often exaggerated, it is nonetheless a grievous mistake to underestimate the importance of democratic institutions in the domain of the state. It is similarly a mistake to underestimate the importance of authoritarian corporate institutions in the daily lives of working people. To be sure, democratic structures

do not escape Robert Michels's "iron law" that organizational imperatives create a thrust toward oligarchy. But Michels's "law" is neither iron nor a law. At
most it is a universal tendency in human organizations; and it is often offset, if never wholly nullified,
by the universal tendency toward personal and group
autonomy and the displacement of strictly hierarchical controls by at least some degree of mutual control. It is not unreasonable to expect that democratic
structures in governing the workplace would satisfy
the criteria of the democratic process neither markedly worse nor markedly better than democratic structures in the government of the state.

Conclusion

My arguments in this chapter have shown, I think,
that the main objections to democratizing economic
enterprises are not adequately supported by analysis
and evidence. It is not true that self-governing enterprises would violate a superior right to private ownership. It is not true that the assumptions justifying
the democratic process in the government of the state
do not apply to economic enterprises. Nor is it true
that democracy in an economic enterprise would be a
sham. If these objections are invalid, then a country
committed to the goals I described in Chapter 3 would
choose to extend democracy to economic enterprises.
The prevailing view among the people of such a
country might be something like this:
If democracy is justified in governing the state,

then it is also justified in governing economic enterprises. What is more, if it cannot be justified in governing economic enterprises, we do not quite see how
it can be justified in governing the state. Members
of any association for whom the assumptions of the
democratic process are valid have a *right* to govern
themselves by means of the democratic process. If, as
we believe, those assumptions hold among us, not
only for the government of the state but also for the
internal government of economic enterprises, then
we have a *right* to govern ourselves democratically
within our economic enterprises. Of course, we do
not expect that the introduction of the democratic
process in the government of economic enterprises
will make them perfectly democratic or entirely over-
come the tendencies toward oligarchy that seem to be
inherent in all large human organizations, including
the government of the state. But just as we support
the democratic process in the government of the state
despite substantial imperfections in practice, so we
support the democratic process in the government
of economic enterprises despite the imperfections we
expect in practice. We therefore see no convincing
reasons why we should not exercise our right to the
democratic process in the government of enterprises,
just as we have already done in the government of the
state. And we intend to exercise that right.

5

Ownership, Leadership, and Transition

By committing itself to a system of self-governing enterprises, a democratic people would take an important step toward attaining the goals of political equality, justice, efficiency, and liberty, both political and economic. They would, of course, continue to face many problems that this structural change would not resolve or even ameliorate. These—the problems of any complex society in a complex world—are naturally beyond the scope of my concerns here.

For example, it seems obvious that a system of self-governing enterprises of the kind described here would still require the central government to exercise authority over many important matters: military and foreign affairs, fiscal and monetary policy, social security and medical care, regulation of externalities judged harmful in comparison with regulatory costs (food, drugs, pollution, etc.), and so on. It might also be desirable for the central government to adopt and implement policies bearing on investment, savings, general economic growth, and sectoral growth or decline. Finally the central government would need to ensure relative ease of entry of firms, not only for the sake of fairness but also to prevent monopolistic exploitation of consumers. Thus a system of self-governing enterprises, no matter what their form of ownership, would not reduce the central government to a mere nightwatchman practicing a laissez-faire policy. Nor would such a system prove to be functionally equivalent either to a Proudhonian anarchist society based on autonomous associations of workers, a market, and free contracts, or to a society decomposed into completely independent and self-sufficient communes.[1]

Four problems, however, are particularly germane to the argument that self-governing firms could make a significant contribution to a democratic society's goals.

Fairness

Although what constitutes a proper standard of equity or fairness in the distribution of economic re-

1. Even in Yugoslavia, divesting the central government of control over fiscal and monetary policy left it with inadequate means for combatting inflation, unemployment, foreign trade deficits, and individual and regional inequalities in wealth and incomes. As Dirlam and Plummer remark, "The 1971 constitutional amendments made the functions of the central government so limited that it would be difficult to imagine Professor Milton Friedman or William Buckley, Jr., withholding their approval" (1973, 186).

sources is endlessly debatable, it would be very hard to develop a reasoned argument that the prevailing distribution of wealth and income in the United States satisfies defensible standards of equity. Few people, in fact, attempt to justify economic inequality as equitable. Even Robert Nozick, who perhaps among recent writers advances the strongest argument against governmental interference with existing property rights, conspicuously avoids doing so. Yet many people who might agree that the prevailing distribution is inequitable would justify it as necessary to efficiency, growth, and full employment. Even among those who hold that the high degree of economic inequality now prevailing is not strictly necessary to ensure business performance, many would agree that because of trade-offs between equity and efficiency, any justifiable redistribution would still have to fall considerably short of reasonable standards of equity (Okun 1975).

In an economy like that of the United States at present, economic performance does seem to require forgoing a very large measure of distributive justice. But if, as I have just suggested, an economy of self-governing enterprises, though by no means fully self-regulating, would make it easier to disperse income and wealth much more widely, then it would also be more equitable. To be sure, even if all enterprises were self-governing, the resulting distribution would not satisfy moderately strong standards of fairness—for example, John Rawls's proposal that no departure from equality in distribution should be permitted unless it improves the lot of the worst-off (Rawls 1971).

If a country were to adopt self-governing enterprises as its model, therefore, its people might also want to see whether they could agree on some general principles of equity in distribution, however rough these principles might be. In applying the principles—by means of taxes and transfers, for example—they would no doubt want to consider possible conflicts between distributive fairness and other important values, including efficiency and growth. But since it would be foolish for me to try to prescribe here the specific solutions a country ought to adopt, much less to predict the pragmatic solutions it would be likely to adopt, I shall not do so.

The important point is that major inequalities in wealth and income in countries like the United States do not flow from interfirm or interindustry wage differentials. They are caused primarily by two other factors: a highly concentrated ownership of property and very large payments to top corporate executives whose decisions are, for all practical purposes, independent of all effective external controls. By dispersing income from ownership more broadly and by bringing executive salaries and bonuses into line, a system of self-governing enterprises would produce a more equitable distribution of wealth and income. By enacting inheritance taxes large enough to prevent the hereditary transmission of wealth, a country could provide a still fairer distribution of life chances among all its citizens.

While a system of self-governing enterprises would not be sufficient to create a perfectly just society, it would enable a country to enjoy a far greater measure of distributive justice than Americans are likely to achieve under their present system of corporate capitalism.

Ownership

How should self-governing enterprises be owned? Four possibilities are particularly relevant: individual ownership by members of an enterprise; cooperative ownership of an enterprise by all its employees; state ownership; or ownership by "society."

Individual ownership. In some producer cooperatives each member owns one share in the firm; owning a share entitles the worker to one vote. This arrangement upholds the principle of one person, one vote, and together with other features provides a basis for democratic control over decisions. Unlike firms in which employees own shares in varying amounts and accumulate votes proportional to shares owned, then, the ownership of a single share and thus a single vote respects democratic criteria.

However, as David Ellerman has argued, worker cooperatives based on share ownership may confront a fatal dilemma: If they are financially unsuccessful, they go under; but if they are successful, as the worker-owned plywood cooperatives of the Pacific Northwest have been—indeed spectacularly so—then their shares become so valuable that prospective new members often cannot afford to buy their way in,[2]

2. "In the better plywood co-ops, a share can be priced in the $60,000 to $80,000 range" (Ellerman 1982, 15).

while members who want to leave the company, particularly on retirement, will prefer to sell their shares to the highest bidder, a process that may lead to a takeover by outsiders and destruction of the cooperative (Ellerman 1982; Zwerdling 1980, 95–104).

Furthermore, if the high market value of the shares excludes potential new members, a cooperative may be undermined in a more subtle way. Because members have not wanted to dilute the value of their shares to make it possible for new members to join, some of the plywood cooperatives (like some of the Israeli kibbutzim) have resorted to hiring wage laborers who, not being members, are distinctly second-class citizens in the enterprise (Zwerdling, 102–3).

Cooperative ownership. To remedy this difficulty and at the same time to affirm the cooperative nature of an economic enterprise, Ellerman and others contend that the workers in a firm should own it cooperatively as a group, a solution adopted by the Mondragon cooperatives in Spain (Thomas and Logan 1982, 7, 149–61; Ellerman 1982, 13–17). Under this scheme, the rights pertaining to ownership are not distributed to individual workers but are vested in the workers as a collectivity. As in any territorial democratic unit, the rights of citizenship in the enterprise are determined not by ownership but by *membership*. Just as citizenship in a democratic country entitles one to full and equal rights as a member of the polity, but does not entitle one to claim ownership of an individual share of the country's wealth, so too in a cooperatively owned enterprise members have full and equal rights but cannot lay claim to a share in the assets or net worth of the firm to dispose of as they choose. Thus instead of receiving transferable shares of stock, each enterprise-citizen is entitled to an "internal account" to which an allotted share of surplus revenues (after wages and other costs, of course) is allocated. Workers might be required to pay a fee in order to acquire membership in the cooperative, in which case their fee creates an initial balance in their internal accounts.[3] At the close of an accounting period, such as a year, the surplus (or loss) is allocated and credited (or debited) to the internal account of each employee.

If the cooperative prospers, the value of the internal accounts, of course, increases. Although these balances, unlike stock certificates, are nontransferable, members are ordinarily entitled to draw on them, within limits designed to protect liquidity. Thus an employee who leaves or retires will not be faced with the task of finding a buyer for his share, as in the plywood cooperatives, but will be able to withdraw the balance, perhaps over a period of several years.

State ownership.   Another alternative is the familiar socialist solution of state ownership. This alternative is, however, clouded by the history of state ownership both in socialist thought and in practice. For the arguments given by socialists and others to justify state ownership ordinarily have also justified denying

3. As of 1982 in the Mondragon Cooperatives "the fee is around $5,000, with about 25% down and the remainder being paid by payroll deductions over a two-year period. On average, the entry fee covers about 10% of the costs of creating the job" (Ellerman 1982, 10).

to state-owned firms the degree of autonomy that self-governing enterprises would need. Thus after a decade or more of debate over the extent of worker participation in nationalized industries, in 1944–45 the British Labour party flatly rejected the notion that workers were entitled to participate directly in governing state-owned firms (Dahl 1947).

As support for bureaucratic socialism has declined, however, some socialists have considered the possibility of combining state ownership with worker control. David Miller proposes that after acquiring ownership of an industry the state could then lease the firms to the employees, who could then operate them as self-governing enterprises (Miller 1977, 475) Among other advantages this solution symbolizes the public nature of economic enterprises, in contrast to ownership by employees, whether individually or co-operatively, which still retains a strong flavor of private ownership. Symbolic effects are not necessarily trivial, and if a system of self-governing enterprises were inaugurated by a socialist party in a country with a relatively strong socialist tradition, this solution might be attractive.

Symbolic state ownership, however, has its own difficulties. If, on the one hand, state ownership were *purely* symbolic, then no legal rights whatsoever would be vested in the state, and the government would possess no authority to intervene directly in the activities of the firm to protect the general, public, or social interest. A government could always intervene, of course, by general legislation; but presumably it could do that even without symbolic ownership. If, on the other hand, state ownership were to convey legal authority to intervene *directly*, the autonomy of the firm would tend to be undermined. For in those circumstances it is unlikely that an initial commitment to permit firms to operate independently of the government would long be honored. Given legislative, executive, and bureaucratic pressures to protect the public interest, it is difficult to see how enterprises would avoid becoming politicized and transformed essentially into government agencies. In the end, then, state ownership might prove to be far from symbolic, while self-government would have become so. A solution intended to avoid bureaucratic socialism might instead drift steadily toward it.

Social ownership.[4]   According to "the most famous legislative act of the postwar era in Yugoslavia," later incorporated into the 1963 constitution,

> the State ceased to be the formal owner of the means of production, which became "social property." The workers in each enterprise became, in effect, trustees of the share of this socially owned property committed to their hands in the form of machinery, buildings, etc., exercising their trusteeship through elective organs: workers' councils . . . and management boards.
>
> *(Rusinow 1977, 58)*

4. A special form of social ownership, not discussed here, is by trade unions, as with Histadrut in Israel or, much more indirectly, the Employee Investment Funds in Sweden.

Because the employees of a firm do not own its assets but hold them in trust for the society, they cannot, for example, sell off the assets for their own benefit (Dirlam and Plummer 1973, 22). But since Yugoslav society is an entity with no means of acting except through its specific institutions, all the rights, powers, and privileges ordinarily associated with ownership must be lodged in specific institutions. Thus social ownership cannot escape what Najdan Pasic calls "the basic dilemma of public ownership . . . [and] therefore the basic dilemma of socialism: who controls the great economic power materialized in public property and social capital?" (Pasic, in Rusinow, 328). Among the institutions that speak authoritatively on this question in Yugoslavia, the Party and the government of the state—whether of the federation or of the republics—are crucially important. Because the structure, duties, and authority of the self-managed enterprises are determined by statutory and constitutional law, sovereign authority over the enterprises seems to rest de jure with the state and de facto with the leadership of Party and state. As a result, ownership of enterprises by "society" is almost entirely symbolic. Since even the prohibition against selling off assets is enforced by the state, here too the distinction between state and social ownership is shadowy.[5]

5. "Business consideration may dictate that some of the assets be sold, but the amounts realized must be kept for use of the enterprise. If the enterprise fails, liquidation can take place, but only under public supervision" (Dirlam and Plummer 1973, 22).

However, because the Party-state leadership has since 1950 created and maintained one of the most decentralized economies in the world, it might be contended that Yugoslavia rebuts my previous argument about the probable dynamics of state ownership. The paradox of the Yugoslav system is that this unusually decentralized economy, which not only permits but also probably achieves a higher degree of democratic control *within* economic enterprises than any other economic system in the world, was imposed and continues to be enforced by a nondemocratic regime. Yugoslavia is thus a mirror image of Western democratic countries: in Yugoslavia the democratic process is required in the governments of economic enterprises but not, or at least not much, in the government of state; in democratic countries, the democratic process is required in the government of the state, but not, or at least not much, in the governments of economic enterprises.

Self-management, originally imposed in Yugoslavia in 1950 for a mixture of pragmatic and ideological reasons, may now be so firmly entrenched that the Party-state leadership could not abolish it without destroying its own legitimacy. Even so, as Dennison Rusinow's detailed account of the rapidly changing Yugoslav experiment from 1948 to 1974 reveals, the dominant role in deciding, more or less unilaterally, what the fundamental political and economic structures of Yugoslavia are to be is retained by the leaders of Party and state, who ordinarily act in and through the Party Congresses. To be sure, social groups, interests, ideologies (within the broad rubric of Marxism), and national identities are often reflected both within the party and in legislative assemblies of the localities, provinces, republics, and the federation. Yet the Party-state leadership has never tolerated organized opposition to its policies, programs, or ideology, or submitted itself to open electoral competition (cf. Rusinow, 261, 330–32, 346).

The example of Yugoslavia suggests three conclusions. First, we cannot infer from Yugoslavia's experience what the dynamics of "social" ownership would be in a system with the range of political rights, pressure groups, parties, ideologies, and institutions characteristic of countries governed by systems of polyarchy. Second, because the rights, powers, and privileges of ownership cannot be directly exercised by "society" but must be vested in a society's institutions, in practice "social" ownership guarantees that leaders who control the government of the state will play a powerful role in shaping the institutions of self-management. Third, "social" ownership does not automatically solve the problem, as Pasic puts it, of "how to prevent self-management from perverting 'social property' into 'group property' through appropriation of effective ownership rights by the professional cadres or even the workers who [manage] it" (in Rusinow, 328). In one sense, every democratic unit is "private" in relation to other units, even more inclusive ones. Insofar as an economic unit is governed by its workers, it cannot be governed by others. Thus in Yugoslavia "social ownership" is effectively converted into the cooperative ownership of the workers in the particular unit. How much would it actually change things, then, if the Yugoslav constitution were to prescribe cooperative rather than social ownership of economic entities?

Advantages of cooperative ownership. Cooperative ownership avoids the problems arising from the need to dispose of individually owned shares, as in the plywood co-ops; yet like individual ownership it provides more protection for the autonomy of the firm against bureaucratic control by the state than would state or, in all likelihood, "social" ownership.

State and social ownership intensify one additional problem that is rarely confronted explicitly: What constitutes an appropriate entity for self-government? Quite beyond the question of workplace democracy, in democratic theory generally the problem of the unit is quite formidable; indeed, it may admit of no satisfactory theoretical solution (Dahl 1983). In any case, the problem must be faced if economic enterprises are to be democratic. Concretely, if "enterprises" were to be self-governing, what would constitute an "enterprise"? If a "workplace" is to be democratic, what is the "workplace"? Often a self-governing enterprise could easily be defined at the outset, particularly if it is converted from an existing firm as in cases like the Vermont Asbestos Group, South Bend Lathe, or Hyatt-Clark Industries, Inc., which was converted from General Motors' New Departure Hyatt Bearings division.

But suppose certain workers within an enterprise claim a right to form their own independent, self-governing unit? Must such a claim be granted automatically? Why so? Must their claim not satisfy certain criteria? If so, which ones? Imagine that in the Widget Producers Co-op a unit that makes hardware for the widgets is highly capital intensive. The workers in the hardware unit wish to form an independent hardware co-op. What is more crucial, they also want to assume full control of the machinery and equipment for making hardware. Are they automatically entitled to claim the Widget Co-op's capital equipment for their own use? Or must they pay for it, say, from their own revenues?

Under either state or social ownership, criteria for a suitable unit would have to be established by law and enforced by the state—rather as the National Labor Relations Board (NLRB) must determine what constitutes an appropriate unit for collective bargaining. In Yugoslavia, the Constitution of 1974

in effect destroyed the enterprise as it had existed since 1950, completing the gradual evolution of "work units," created in the late 1950s and since 1971 called BOALs (Basic Organizations of Associated Labor), into the central legal entity of the economic system. . . . Net income from economic activities was now BOAL income, its use and distribution with few restrictions under each BOAL's control; the enterprise had no income of its own.

(Rusinow, 328–29)

As with the NLRB and the collective bargaining unit, the determination of what constitutes an appropriate economic entity for self-government is not so much beyond practical solution as simply difficult and bur-

densome: the NLRB has had to create a vast and formidable body of case law on the matter of the proper
bargaining unit.

Cooperative ownership offers the possibility of a
less legalistic solution to this problem. Suppose that
any group of workers would be legally entitled to
become an independent, self-governing cooperative
provided they could acquire the assets they need for
their work, by purchase, lease, rental, or whatever.
If, for example, the workers in the hardware unit
could arrange to buy the capital equipment they need
from the Widget Co-op by means of long-term loans
repayable from surplus revenues (as occurred under
the ESOP financing package for the Rath Packing
Company, Hyatt-Clark Industries, and others), they
would be entitled to do so. An independent hardware
co-op might contract to supply gadgets to the Widget
Co-op, just as Hyatt-Clark contracted to supply bearings to General Motors. Thus simply by negotiating
a contract, the parties could settle a complex question
that under state or social ownership would require a
decision by a regulatory agency of the state.

Capitalism or socialism?   I imagine that some people
will not know which of these forms of ownership
they prefer until they first answer what they assume
to be a prior question: Is it capitalist or is it socialist?

But is this question fundamentally important?
Surely the key question is not how a proposal is to be
labeled but whether and how much it would help a
people to realize their fundamental values. No doubt
some ideologues will disapprove of a system of self-

governing enterprises unless it can be classified as capitalist; others will disapprove unless it can be classified as socialist. Alas for such simple and rigid ideological views, in the case of cooperative ownership the correct answer is either, both, and neither.

Under cooperative ownership the members of a self-governing enterprise would—as individuals—lack most of the rights thought essential to private property, such as rights to possess, use, manage, rent, sell, alienate, destroy, or transmit portions of the enterprise. Of course, individual shareholders in a private firm also lack those rights as regards the property of the firm; they possess them only as regards their own shares. In a self-governing enterprise, the members might possess all these rights collectively; but they would not possess them individually. In that sense, a cooperatively owned self-governing enterprise would be both public and private: public in relation to its individual members and private in relation to all nonmembers. If you were a member your share of the surplus would belong exclusively to you in the sense that you and only you would be entitled to it; but you could not sell or otherwise transmit your share. Your share would be your personal property, so to speak, but not your private property. Viewed from one perspective, then, a self-governing system would look something like capitalism; viewed from another, it would look more like decentralized socialism.

Attempting to locate such a system within one of these two conventional categories will not, I think, prove fruitful. Speaking for myself, I would not be greatly distressed if advocates of capitalism were to view it as a new and better form of capitalism, and socialists as a new and better form of socialism. But I know that theological disputes cannot be dismissed so cavalierly.

Leadership

The question of leadership has always been difficult for advocates of democracy, and not least for its theorists. To portray a democratic order without leaders is a conspicuous distortion of all historical experience; but to put them into the picture is even more troublesome. Whether by definition, by implication, or simply as a fact, leaders, as individuals, exercise more direct influence on many decisions than ordinary individual citizens. Thus the superior influence of leaders violates strict criteria for political equality. Given the influence of leadership and a strict interpretation of democracy, many people find it tempting to follow Michels in arguing from the inevitability of political inequality to a non sequitur, the inevitability of oligarchy.

Because leadership is a general problem of democratic theory and practice we should neither expect nor require self-governing enterprises to solve it better, either in theory or in practice, than other kinds of democratic organizations, including local and national governments. Although some writers have tried to justify workplace democracy on the ground that it will be *more* participatory, *more* egalitarian, and generally *more* democratic than the democratic process applied to the state has so far proved to be, the justification given in this book does not hinge upon such a claim. For my argument is that self-government in work need not be justified entirely by its consequences, for, as in the state, it is justified as a matter of right. And just as the imperfections of the democratic process in the government of the state do not justify abandoning democracy in favor of guardianship, so its imperfections in economic enterprises would not justify our accepting guardianship as better in the government of economic enterprises.

Yet it is of little comfort to say that people have a right to govern themselves disastrously: in such circumstances a people might prefer, and choose, not to exercise that right. In self-governing firms, how would the problem of leadership display itself? Up to this point we have discovered no reason to expect self governing enterprises to be more poorly governed than American corporations. For example, in selecting executives, employees should be at least as competent as either stockholders or cooptative management in firms with hierarchical, authoritarian structures, and there are cogent arguments that employees in self-governing enterprises would do a better job of selecting managers. (I shall return to this point in a moment.) No doubt executives, because of their special skills and opportunities, would tend to exercise more influence on many matters than rank-and-file members, and to this extent self-governing firms would violate strict criteria of political equality and the democratic process. But then so do virtually all other democratic organizations, and there is no reason to think that self-governing enterprises would satisfy democratic criteria less than other organizations, including local and national governments.

However, these conclusions by no means cause the problem of leadership to disappear. In particular, any proposal for a system of self-governing enterprises must confront the question of innovation. How are new products to be invented, new processes developed, new systems produced and marketed? How are new economic organizations to be created—whether firms, units within firms, subcontractors, or the equivalent of the Yugoslav BOALs? These are the tasks of entrepreneurship—or, within firms, what one writer has called "intrapreneurship" (*The Economist*, 17–23 April 1982, 68 and 67–72 generally). How are they to be performed? As long as self-governing enterprises remain a small part of an economy, the task of entrepreneurial innovation might be left to others, even though that neglect would hardly promise well for the growth of the self-governing sector. But if self-governing enterprises were ever to become the standard form, they would have to take on the job themselves.

If innovation were to prove a continuing problem in an economy of self-governing firms, then entrepreneurship could be cultivated by offering special short-term incentives. An organizer of a new firm, for example, might have a grace period of five years or so within which the firm would be exempt from any requirement of self-governance. At the end of the grace period, however, the firm would have to be converted into a self-governing enterprise, possibly under a standard national charter.

There are, however, at least three reasons for thinking that self-governing enterprises could handle the challenge successfully. First, self-government may be particularly suitable for smaller firms, and smaller firms are the seedbed of innovation. Despite the mystique of the giant manufacturing firm, neither manufacturing nor the giant corporation represents the growing edge of a modern economy. Since the mid 1960s, the thousand largest firms in the United States have reduced their labor force, while "more than the whole of the [net new] fifteen million private-sector jobs created since then have come in smaller firms"— "more than the whole" because the number of jobs created during the period exceeded the net remaining at the end of the period. In addition, "[the] majority of new extra jobs at any one time [are] in firms less than five years old, even though more than half of new small American firms disappear out of business in their first five years" (*Economist*, 68). In the United States, Japan, and Britain between 1967 and 1976, manufacturing firms with two hundred or more employees reduced employment, while in these three countries small firms grew. In fact, in both Japan and the United States the fastest rate of employment growth took place in firms with fewer than ten employees. And more than two-thirds of the world's major inventions over the past fifty years have been discovered by individuals or small businesses (*Economist*, 67–68).

Second, the style of management typical of the

large American corporation (and many smaller ones
as well) is ill-suited to innovation and growth. Authoritarian leadership in the government of a firm
suffers from many of the practical defects of authoritarian leadership in the government of the state. At
the one extreme, authoritarian leaders stifle criticism,
suppress opponents, cut themselves off from intelligence, and, because effective checks to their power
are lacking, adopt and adhere to policies that lead to
failure. Though leaders in the automobile industry
possess far less power than rulers in authoritarian
states, and their mistakes have been infinitely less
costly, their insistence on building traditional large
cars in the face of strong indications of consumer
preference having shifted to smaller cars resembles
other, more famous failures of authoritarian leadership, such as Stalin's disastrous collectivization of
agriculture, Hitler's invasion of the Soviet Union,
Mao's Cultural Revolution, and Castro's re-creation
of a one-crop economy.

At the other extreme, leaders with strong hierarchical authority are inhibited from gaining an adequate understanding of their most precious resource
for productivity, innovation, and growth: their own
work force. Because the remoteness of authoritarian
leadership in a firm is combined with bureaucrati-
zation, reliance on technical analysis, insistence on
abstract criteria of performance, and the pursuit of
short-term profits to enhance the reputation, salaries,
and bonuses of the executives, the orthodox hierarchical management of American firms has become a
prescription for economic decline. By contrast, self-

government would virtually compel managers to concern themselves, as Japanese executives tend to do, with the loyalty, welfare, and productivity of their employees.

Our present system hardly begins to tap the potential of the labor force for energy and creativity. How close to a maximum contribution, within humane limits, does the average American employee perform? Whether the actual figure is 1 percent or 20 percent, it is surely far short of what is possible—as the gap in performance between poorly motivated and highly motivated workers has shown in a thousand studies. Is it not reasonable to think that democratic leadership will go further in helping to achieve that potential than authoritarian leadership can ever do?

The third reason for believing that self-governing enterprises could deal successfully with the problem of innovation is the Empresarial (or entrepreneurial) Division of the cooperative bank created by the Mondragon Cooperative Movement. The cooperative bank (Caja Laboral Popular [CLP]) has been a highly successful financial institution that in less than a quarter century has become Spain's twenty-sixth largest bank, with 120 branches, over a thousand workers, and a half-million customers. Its ability to accumulate savings has been so great that by 1982 its lending capacity had begun to exceed the needs of the cooperatives (Ellerman 1982, 21).

Among other activities, the CLP lends funds to new cooperative enterprises, which are created in the following way. Within the CLP, the Products Department of the Empresarial Division continually explores possibilities for new markets and products. These "prefeasibility studies" are assembled in a "product bank," which is kept current for reference by new enterprises. Typically, a new enterprise is begun by a group of workers who approach the CLP with a proposal for a product (which may or may not already be in the product bank) and a leader or promoter-manager whom they have designated to work with the CLP. For eighteen months to two years the promoter-manager then works with an advisor in the Products Department to perform a feasibility study, perhaps revising the group's original ideas as to a marketable product.[6] If the proposal then looks promising, the CLP enters into a contract with the group, and the Promotions and Intervention Department of the Empresarial Division helps the group through the difficult process of launching their cooperative. Under the guidance of the Empresarial Division, that process has proved to be strikingly successful:

Even allowing for cultural and economic differences, the record of starting over a hundred firms, including some of the largest producers in Spain, in the last 25 years with only one failure must be seen as a quantum leap over the quality and type of entrepreneurship represented in America where 80 to 90 percent of all new small businesses fail within five years.

(Ellerman 1982, 4)

6. In Ellerman's judgment "the Mondragon feasibility studies are considerably more sophisticated and reliable than even the better ones produced by, say, American MBA's" (1982, 32).

Transition

A system of self-governing enterprises along the lines I have sketched would, I believe, appeal to a people committed to equality with liberty.

A wise people, however, would wish for evidence more convincing than abstract arguments seasoned with a few examples of the sort presented here. A practical people would want to know how such a system could best be brought about. A people committed to democracy and political liberty would want to ensure that the transition would respect the democratic process and primary political rights.

Two possibilities would no doubt occur to such a people. One would be to facilitate the takeover by employees of firms in financial difficulty. For example, local and central government agencies could assist the transition with loans, guarantees, and reduction or remission of taxes. The expansion in the number of self-governing firms brought about in this fashion would then provide additional experience with which to appraise advantages and disadvantages, and to indicate a need for changes in the standard structure or in public policies. The experience, however, would be rather lopsided—taking over a failing firm is hardly a fair test. It would therefore be desirable to undertake a more vigorous and valid experiment by bringing about self-government in a few typical firms in several industries. A country might do so, for example, by government takeovers followed by the sale of a firm to employees and reconstitution as a self-governing enterprise, and by the establishment of an adequately funded bank for self-governing enterprises.

If broader experience were to confirm the initial judgment, a country could then proceed to move much more boldly. Drawing on the Swedish and Danish proposals, for example, the legislature could enact a law requiring that a percentage of revenues, profits, or payrolls be set aside, partly to fund the bank for self-governing enterprises, partly to bring a steady transition to self-governing enterprises. By means of income and inheritance taxes, the residual concentration of wealth could gradually be dispersed. In this way a country could in due time bring about an economic order that, while operating within a relatively stable structure of laws and regulations, would generate a wide distribution of authority and economic resources, and thus provide an appropriate social and economic foundation for a democratic order.

Epilogue

Tocqueville believed that equality, desirable though it may be, poses a standing threat to liberty. But if self-government by means of the democratic process is a fundamental, even an inalienable right; if the exercise of that inalienable right necessarily requires a substantial number of more particular rights, which are therefore also fundamental and inalienable; and if a certain equality of condition is necessary to the political equality entailed in the democratic process, then the conflict, if there be one, is not simply between equality and liberty. It is, rather, a conflict between fundamental liberties of a special kind, the liberties people enjoy by virtue of governing themselves through the democratic process, and other liberties of a different kind.

Among these other liberties is economic liberty, which Americans have generally understood to include a personal and inalienable right to property. Applied to an economic enterprise, ownership carries with it a right to govern the enterprise, within broad limits, of course, set by the government of the state. Transferred from the operation of farms and small businesses to the large corporation, ownership rights have given legality and legitimacy to undemocratic governments that intrude deeply into the lives of many people, and most of all the lives of those who work under the rulership of authorities over whom they exercise scant control. Thus a system of government Americans view as intolerable in governing the state has come to be accepted as desirable in governing economic enterprises.

I have sketched here an alternative form of government for economic enterprises that holds promise of eliminating, or at least reducing, this contradiction. A system of self-governing enterprises would be one part of a system of equalities and liberties in which both would, I believe, be stronger, on balance, than they can be in a system of corporate capitalism. But whether many Americans will find this vision attractive I cannot say. For we Americans have always been torn between two conflicting visions of what American society is and ought to be. To summarize them oversimply, one is a vision of the world's first and grandest attempt to realize democracy, political equality, and political liberty on a continental scale. The other is a vision of a country where unrestricted liberty to acquire unlimited wealth would produce the world's most prosperous society. In the first, American ideals are realized by the achievement of democracy, political equality, and the fundamental political rights of all citizens in a country of vast size and diversity. In the second, American ideals are realized by the protection of property and of opportunities to prosper materially and to grow wealthy. In the first view, the right to self-government is among the most fundamental of all human rights, and, should they conflict, is superior to the right to property. In the second, property is the superior, self-government the subordinate right.

As a people we are divided among ourselves in the strength of our commitment to these conflicting ideals; and many Americans are divided within themselves. I cannot say whether a people so divided possesses the firmness of purpose and the clarity of vision to assert the priority of democracy, political equality, and the political rights necessary to self-government over established property rights, economic inequality, and undemocratic authority within corporate enterprises.

Bibliography

Allen, William S. 1965. *The Nazi Seizure of Power*. Chicago: Quadrangle Books.

Becker, Lawrence C. 1977. *Property Rights*. London: Routledge & Kegan Paul.

Bennett, Leamon J. 1979. "When Employees Run the Company: An Interview with Leamon J. Bennett." *Harvard Business Review* 57 (January–February): 75–90.

Berman, Katrina V. 1982. "The Worker-Owned Plywood Companies." In *Workplace Democracy and Social Change*, edited by Frank Lindenfeld and Joyce Rothschild-Whitt. Boston: Porter Sargent.

Bermeo, Nancy. 1982. "The Revolution Within the Revolution: Workers' Control in Rural Portugal." Ph.D. diss., Yale University.

Bertsch, Gary K., and Obradovic, Josip. n.d. "Power and Responsibility Under Self-Managing Socialism: Leadership Values Among Yugoslav Managers." Mimeo.

Bluestone, Barry. 1980. "Roundtable on Jobs and Industrial Policy." *Working Papers* 7(November–December): 47–59.

Blum, John M., et al. 1963. *The National Experience*. New York: Harcourt Brace.

Botana, Natalio R. 1977. *El orden conservador: La política argentina entre 1880 y 1916*. Buenos Aires: Editorial Sudamericana.

Brest, Paul. 1975. *Process of Constitutional Decisionmaking: Cases and Materials*. Boston: Little, Brown.

Clayre, Alasdair, ed. 1980. *The Political Economy of the Third Sector: Cooperation and Participation.* Oxford: Oxford University Press.

Comisso, Ellen Turkish. 1979. *Workers' Control Under Plan and Market.* New Haven: Yale University Press.

Commons, John R., et al. 1936. *History of Labor in the United States.* Vol. 2. New York: Macmillan.

Comptroller General. 1980. *Report to the Committee on Finance of the United States Senate, Employee Stock Ownership Plans: Who Benefits Most in Closely Held Companies?* Gaithersburg, Md.: U.S. General Accounting Office.

Dahl, Robert A. 1947. "Workers' Control of Industry and the British Labor Party." *American Political Science Review* 41(October): 875–900.

———. 1971. *Polyarchy: Participation and Opposition.* New Haven: Yale University Press.

———. 1979. "Procedural Democracy." In *Philosophy, Politics, and Society, Fifth Series,* edited by Peter Laslett and James Fishkin. New Haven: Yale University Press.

———. 1982. *Dilemmas of Pluralist Democracy.* New Haven: Yale University Press.

———. 1983. "Federalism and the Democratic Process." In *Liberal Democracy,* Nomos 25, edited by J. Roland Pennock and John W. Chapman. New York: New York University Press.

Denison, Edward. 1974. *Accounting for U.S. Economic Growth, 1929–1969.* Washington, D.C.: Brookings Institution.

Dirlam, Joel B. 1979. "Some Problems of Workers' Self-Management Specific to Integrated, Cyclical, Oligopolistic Industries: Steel." *Economic Analysis and Workers' Management* 13 (3): 339–54.

Dirlam, Joel B., and Plummer, James L. 1973. *An Introduction to the Yugoslav Economy.* Columbus, Ohio: Charles E. Merrill.

Drucker, Peter. 1976. *The Unseen Revolution: How Pension Fund Socialism Came to America.* New York: Harper & Row.

Elden, J. Maxwell. 1981. "Political Efficacy at Work." *American Political Science Review* 75(March): 43–58.

Ellerman, David P. 1980a. "Property and Production: An Introduction to the Labor Theory of Property." Somerville, Mass.: Industrial Cooperative Association.

———. 1980b. "Property Theory and Orthodox Economics." In *Essays on the Revival of Political Economy*, edited by Edward J. Nell. Cambridge: Cambridge University Press.

———. 1982. "The Socialization of Entrepreneurialism: The Empresarial Division of the Caja Laboral Popular." Somerville, Mass.: Industrial Cooperative Association.

———. n.d. "The Employment Relation, Property Rights and Organizational Democracy." Somerville, Mass.: Industrial Cooperative Association.

———. n.d. "The Union as the Legitimate Opposition in an Industrial Democracy." Somerville, Mass.: Industrial Cooperative Association.

Estrin, Saul, and Bartlett, William. 1982. "The Effects of Enterprise Self-Management in Yugoslavia: An Empirical Survey." In *Participatory and Self-Managed Firms: Evaluating Economic Performance*, edited by Derek Jones and Jan Svejnar. Lexington, Mass.: D. C. Heath.

Fishkin, James S. 1979. *Tyranny and Legitimacy.* New Haven: Yale University Press.

Germani, Gino. 1969. "The Transition to a Mass Democracy in Argentina." In *Reform and Revolution*, edited by Arpad von Lazar and Robert R. Kaufman. Boston: Allyn & Bacon.

Gil, Federico G. 1966. *The Political System of Chile.* Boston: Houghton Mifflin.

Gillespie, Charles G. 1982. "The Breakdown of Democracy in Uruguay: Alternative Political Models." Paper presented at the Twenty-first World Congress of the International Political Science Association, Rio de Janeiro, 9–14 August 1982.

Gonzalez, Luis E. 1982a. "Uruguay 1980–81: Una Apertura Inesperada." Paper presented at the tenth national meeting of the Latin American Studies Association, Washington, D.C., 4–6 March 1982.

———. 1982b. "Ideology, Party Identification, and the Prospects for Democracy in Uruguay." Department of Political Science, Yale University. Typescript.

Greenberg, Edward S. 1981. "Industrial Self-Management and Political Attitudes." *American Political Science Review* 75(March): 29–42.

Gunn, Christopher. 1981. The Fruits of Rath: A New Model of Self-Management." *Working Papers* 7(March–April): 7–21.

Gustaffson, Bo. 1983. "Co-Determination and Wage Earners' Funds: The Swedish Experience." Uppsala: Uppsala University.

Hagtvet, Bernt. 1980. "The Theory of Mass Society and the Collapse of the Weimar Republic: A Re-Examination." In *Who Were the Fascists? Social Roots of European Fascism*, edited by Stein U. Larsen, Bernt Hagtvet, and Jan P. Myklebust. Bergen: Universitetsforlaget.

Herman, Edward S. 1981. *Corporate Control, Corporate Power.* Cambridge: Cambridge University Press.

Hirschman, Albert. 1970. *Exit, Voice, and Loyalty.* Cambridge, Mass.: Harvard University Press.

Hofstadter, Richard. 1965. *The Paranoid Style in American Politics: And Other Essays.* New York: Knopf.

Jay, Peter. 1980. "The Workers' Cooperative Economy." In *The Political Economy of the Third Sector: Cooperation and Participation*, edited by Alasdair Clayre. Oxford: Oxford University Press.

Jones, Derek, and Svejnar, Jan, eds. 1982. *Participatory and Self-Managed Firms: Evaluating Economic Performance.* Lexington, Mass.: D. C. Heath.

Kornhauser, William. 1959. *The Politics of Mass Society.* New York: Free Press of Glencoe.

Lepsius, M. Rainer. 1978. "From Fragmented Party Democracy to Government by Emergency Decree and National Socialist Takeover: Germany." In *The Breakdown of Democratic Regimes: Crisis, Breakdown, and Requalibrium,* edited by Juan J. Linz and Alfred Stepan. Baltimore: Johns Hopkins University Press.

Lindblom, Charles E. 1977. *Politics and Markets: The World's Political-Economic Systems.* New York: Basic Books.

Linz, Juan J., and Stepan, Alfred. 1978. *The Breakdown of Democratic Regimes: Crisis, Breakdown, and Requalibrium.* Baltimore: Johns Hopkins University Press.

Locke, John. [1689] 1970. *Two Treatises of Government.* 2d ed. Edited by Peter Laslett. Cambridge: Cambridge University Press.

Loomis, Carol L. 1982. "The Madness of Executive Compensation." *Fortune* (July 12): 42–52.

Mason, Ronald. 1982. *Participatory and Workplace Democracy.* Carbondale: Southern Illinois University Press.

Meidner, Rudolf. 1978. *Employee Investment Funds.* London: Allen & Unwin.

Melman, Seymour. 1958. *Decision-Making and Productivity.* Oxford: Basil Blackwell.

Michels, Robert. [1915] 1962. *Political Parties.* New York: Collier Books.

Mill, John Stuart. [1861] 1958. *Considerations on Representative Government.* Edited by Currin U. Shields. New York: Bobbs-Merrill.

Miller, David. 1977. "Socialism and the Market." *Political Theory* 5(November): 473–89.

Ministry of Labour, Denmark. 1973. *Economic Democracy, Introduction and Bill* (translation). Copenhagen.

Morlino, Leonardo. 1980. *Come Cambiano i Regimi Politici.* Milan: Franco Angelo Editore.

Nozick, Robert. 1974. *Anarchy, State, and Utopia.* New York: Basic Books.

Obradovic, Josip. 1970. "Participation and Work Attitudes in Yugoslavia." *Industrial Relations* 9(February): 161–69.

———. 1972. "Distribution of Participation in the Process of Decisionmaking on Problems Related to the Economic Activity of the Company." In *Participation and Self-Management*, edited by Eugen Pusic, vol. 2. Zagreb: Institute for Social Research.

O'Donnell, Guillermo. 1978. "Permanent Crisis and the Failure to Create a Democratic Regime: Argentina, 1955–66." In *The Breakdown of Democratic Regimes: Crisis, Breakdown, and Requalibrium*, edited by Juan J. Linz and Alfred Stepan. Baltimore: Johns Hopkins University Press.

Okun, Arthur M. 1975. *Equality and Efficiency.* Washington, D.C.: Brookings Institution.

Oleszczuk, Thomas. 1973. "Representatives of Workers' Councils." *American Political Science Review* 72:1368–70.

Ortega y Gassett, José. [1930] 1961. *The Revolt of the Masses.* London: Allen & Unwin.

Pateman, Carole. 1970. *Participation and Democratic Theory.* Cambridge: Cambridge University Press.

Pendle, George. 1963. *Uruguay.* 3d ed. Oxford: Oxford University Press.

Peterson, Merrill D., ed. 1966. *Democracy, Liberty, and Property: The State Constitutional Conventions of the 1820's.* Indianapolis: Bobbs-Merrill.

Pusic, Eugen, ed. 1972. *Participation and Self-Management.* Vol. 2. Zagreb: Institute for Social Research.

Rae, Douglas. 1981. *Equalities.* Cambridge, Mass.: Harvard University Press.

Rawls, John. 1971. *A Theory of Justice.* Cambridge, Mass.: Harvard University Press, Belknap Press.

Rusinow, Dennison. 1977. *The Yugoslav Experiment, 1948–1974.* Berkeley and Los Angeles: University of California Press.

Schlatter, Richard. 1951. *Private Property: The History of an Idea.* New Brunswick, N.J.: Rutgers University Press.

Schnitzer, Martin. 1974. *Income Distribution: A Comparative Study of the United States, Sweden, West Germany, East Germany, the United Kingdom, and Japan.* New York: Praeger.

Schweickart, David. 1980. *Capitalism or Worker Control?* New York: Praeger.

Select Committee on Small Business, U.S. Senate. 1979. *The Role of the Federal Government and Employee Ownership of Business.* Washington, D.C.: Government Printing Office.

Selucky, Radoslav. 1979. *Marxism, Socialism, Freedom: Towards a General Democratic Theory of Labour-Management Systems.* New York: St. Martin's Press.

Silk, Leonard, and Vogel, David. 1976. *Ethics and Profits.* New York: Simon & Schuster.

Simmons, John, and Mares, William. 1983. *Working Together.* New York: Knopf.

Smith, James D.; Franklin, Stephen D.; and Wion, Douglas A. 1973. "The Distribution of Financial Assets." Washington, D.C.: The Urban Institute.

Smith, Peter H. 1978. "The Breakdown of Democracy in Argentina, 1916–30." In *The Breakdown of Democratic Regimes: Crisis, Breakdown, and Requalibrium,* edited by Juan J. Linz and Alfred Stepan. Baltimore: Johns Hopkins University Press.

Stepan, Alfred. 1978. *The State and Society: Peru in Comparative Perspective*. Princeton: Princeton University Press.

Thomas, H., and Logan, C. 1982. *Mondragon: An Economic Analysis*. London: Allen & Unwin.

Tocqueville, Alexis de. [1856] 1955. *The Old Regime and the French Revolution*. Garden City, N.Y.: Doubleday.

———. [1835, 1840] 1961. *Democracy in America*. 2 vols. New York: Schocken Books.

Vanek, Jaroslav. 1970. *General Theory of Labor-Managed Market Economies*. Ithaca, N.Y.: Cornell University Press.

———, ed. 1975. *Self-Management, Economic Liberation of Man*. New York: Penguin.

Verba, Sidney; Nie, Norman H.; and Jae-on Kim. 1978. *Participation and Political Equality*. Cambridge: Cambridge University Press.

Verba, Sidney, and Shabad, Goldie. 1978. "Workers' Councils and Political Stratification: The Yugoslav Experience." *American Political Science Review* 72:80–95.

Ward, B. N. 1957. "Workers' Management in Yugoslavia." *Journal of Political Economics* 65(October): 373–86.

———. 1958. "The Firm in Illyria: Market Syndicalism." *American Economic Review* 48(September): 566–689.

———. 1967. *The Socialist Economy: A Study of Organizational Alternatives*. New York: Random House.

Wilde, Alexander W. 1978. "Conversations Among Gentlemen: Oligarchical Democracy in Colombia." In *The Breakdown of Democratic Regimes: Crisis, Breakdown, and Requalibrium*, edited by Juan J. Linz and Alfred Stepan. Baltimore: Johns Hopkins University Press.

Wills, Gary. 1978. *Inventing America: Jefferson's Declaration of Independence*. Garden City, N.Y.: Doubleday.

Witte, John F. 1980. *Democracy, Authority, and Alienation in Work*. Chicago: University of Chicago Press.

Wootton, Graham. 1966. *Workers, Unions, and the State.* London: Routledge & Kegan Paul.

Wright, J. Patrick. 1979. *On A Clear Day You Can See General Motors.* New York: Avon.

Zwerdling, Daniel. 1980. *Workplace Democracy.* New York: Harper & Row.

Index

Adams, John, 1
Africa, 38n
Agrarian democratic republicanism, 3, 71–73, 101
Akontacija (wages, Yugoslavia), 124n
Alienation from work, and self-governing enterprises, 96, 97
Allen, William S., 37
Arendt, Hannah, 37
Argentina, democracy and dictatorship in, 38–44, 49
Aristotle, 69, 87
Associations, role of, in democracies, 22, 23, 45n, 46–47
Athens, classical, liberty in, 20
Atomization, social, 35–36, 37
Australia, 40n, 49
Austria, democracy and dictatorship in, 38–44
Authoritarianism, 35–44

Becker, Lawrence, 81
Belgium, 40n
Berle, Adolf, 119
Blum, John M., 72
BOALs (Basic Organizations of Associated Labor, Yugoslavia), 149, 154
Brazil, democracy and dictatorship in, 38–44
Buckley, William, Jr., 137n
Bureaucratic socialism: efficiency problems of, 131; governance

under, 117–18; resource inequalities in, 60–61; and state ownership of self-governing enterprises, 143. *See also* Socialism

Caja Laboral Popular (CLP), 157–58
Canada, 40n
Capital. *See* Investment
Capitalism: and inequality, 101–2; and ownership of self-governing enterprises, 150–52
Castro, Fidel, 156
Child labor, 15
Chile, democracy and dictatorship in, 38–44
China, People's Republic of, 156
Chrysler Corporation, 123
Church, role of, in Poland, 47
Civil War, American, 53, 74
CLP. *See* Caja Laboral Popular
Collective bargaining, 130, 149–50. *See also* Unions
Colombia, democracy and dictatorship in, 38–44
Conformity, as threat to liberty, 13
Congress, U.S., economic regulation by, 63
Constitution, U.S., 1, 2, 21; and corporate immunity from government regulation, 73; and right to property, 63; and state governments, 11–12

176

Index

Constitutional Convention (U.S.), 1, 2, 21

Control of economic enterprises, 4, 5–6; and political inequality, 54–56

Cooperative ownership of self-governing enterprises, 141–42, 148–50, 151; advantages of, 148–50; Yugoslav social ownership as, 147–48

Coppage v. *Kansas* (1915), 64–65

Corporate capitalism: and agrarian democratic republicanism, 72–73; distribution and concentration of stockholding in, 103n; efficiency problems of, 131; governance of, 117–18; increasing power of, and Supreme Court, 63; lack of moral responsibility of, 99; and political inequality, 55–56; quest for alternatives to, 4; resource inequalities in, 60–61, 74–75; and rewards for property owners, 103; and right to private property, 73–83; utilitarian view of, 82

Corporate property, private ownership of, 77–83

Corporations, 3; democracy in, 133; governance of, 117–20; ownership of, 74–75, 79–80, 119; protected from governmental regulation, 73

Costa Rica, 40n

Credit, access to, and self-governing enterprises, 132

Cultural Revolution, Chinese, 156

Decentralization: in economic order, 89–90; and reconciliation of equality with liberty, 47–48

Decision making in economic enterprises, 113–16

DeLorean, John, 99n

Democracy: breakdown of oligarchical, 41; compared to non-democratic regimes, 18–20; conflict of property with, 68–72; in corporations, 133–34; deviance from standards of, in U.S., 23–24; economic well-being and, 45–46; equality in, 10–12; fragility of, 39–40; as goal of economic order, 84–85; goals of, and self-governing enterprises, 94–107; hostility to, 42; inequalities in, 53; justification of economic governance by, 134–35; and mass-based despotism, 31–44; and property, 65–73; range of political liberties in, 18–20; right to, within firms, 111–35; and rights of majority, 26–29; and rights necessary for self-government, 25–26; self-governing enterprises and, 93–107; sovereignty of majority required for, 9; survival of institutions of, 52–53; threat of equality to liberty in, 44–51; transformation of, into dictatorship, 38–44; as value of economic order, 84; violation of basic liberties in, 20–27. *See also* Democratic process

Democratic process, 56–62; applied to enterprises, 134–35; assumptions about, 57–59, 61–62, 111–12, 113–16; criteria for, 59–62; and enterprise ownership, 83; equality and liberty in, 57–58; fairness principle in, 58–59; and property rights, 62–73; and self-government as right, 161; as type of association, 56–57. *See also* Democracy

Self-governing enterprises, 91–94,
107–10; arguments against,
111–12; capitalist or socialist
ownership of, 150–52; compared with other forms of employee participation, 92–93;
cooperative ownership of, 141–
42, 148–50; and democratic
goals, 94–107; distributive principles of, 106–7; efficiency in,
130–33; employer-employee relations in, 109; fairness of distribution under, 137–40; governmental role in system of,
136–37; and human regeneration, 95–98; leadership of,
152–58; and management skills,
128–30; and means of economic
enterprise, 128–33; meeting of
business ends by, 120–28; and
moral responsibility, 98–101;
nonhierarchical structure of,
112, 116–33; ownership of,
140–52; and political equality,
101–7, 162–63; problems confronted by, 136–60; revenue allocation in, 92; role of unions
in, 116n; and size of enterprise,
155; social ownership of, 144–
48; state ownership of, 142–44;
and strong principle of equality,
116–33; transition to, 159–60;
and values of justice and democracy, 93–94; voting equality
in, 91; wage and salary differentials in, 105–7; worker participation in, justification for,
111–12
Self-government, and property
rights, 64–73, 75–76, 162–63
Self-management, in Yugoslavia,
97, 98, 107–8n, 124, 125n, 131,
146–47
Separation of powers, and recon-

ciliation of equality with liberty,
47–48
Slavery, abolition of, 14, 19, 23, 74
Social Democratic party (Den-
mark), 127–28
Social Democratic party (Sweden), 125–26, 127
Social ownership of self-governing enterprises, 144–48
Social security, 14, 136
Social standing, 3
Socialism: and governance of economic enterprise, 117–18; and
ownership of self-governing enterprises, 150–52. *See also* Bureaucratic socialism
South Bend Lathe Co., 148
Spain, 36, 38–44; workers' cooperatives in, 123–25. *See also*
Mondragon Cooperatives
Stalin, Josef, 156
State: economic regulation by, 63;
ownership of self-governing enterprises by, in Yugoslavia,
144–48
Stockholders: ownership by, separated from control, 119; right
to ownership by, questioned,
79–80
Story, Justin, 75, 109; and right to
property, 67, 69–70, 71, 72
Substantive due process, 63
Suffrage, 22; and development of
dictatorships, 39–40; and property, 67, 69. *See also* Elections;
Voting
Supreme Court, U.S., and right
to private property, 63–65, 73
Sweden, 40n, 125–27, 128,
144n, 160

Terra, Gabriel, 40
Tocqueville, Alexis de: and agrar-

Compositor:	G&S Typesetters, Inc.
Printer and Binder:	IBT
Text:	Bembo
Display:	Bembo